GRIT
IN YOUR
CRAW

THE 8 STRENGTHS YOU NEED
TO SUCCEED IN BUSINESS AND IN LIFE

ROBERT
LUCKADOO

Copyrighted Material

Grit in Your Craw
Copyright © 2015 by Southern Flair Communications

ALL RIGHTS RESERVED
No part of this publication may be reproduced, stored in a retrieval system or transmitted, in any form or by any means—electronic, mechanical, photocopying, recording or otherwise—without prior written permission, except for the inclusion of brief quotations in a review.

For information about this title or to order other books and/or electronic media, contact the publisher:
Southern Flair Communications
Jackson, MS
www.robertluckadoo.com
Robert@robertluckadoo.com

ISBN: 978-0-9907856-0-6 (Print)
      978-0-9907856-1-3 (Ebook)

Printed in the United States of America
Cover and Interior design by: 1106 Design

DEDICATION

I dedicate this book to my wonderful wife, Paula.

You are an inspiration to me for all things big and small. Thank you for all the sacrifices you have made for us and for the endless support you have given to me through each of my endeavors. Not only are you a great partner, but you are truly an inspiration to me and I love you with all my heart!

And to our daughters, Lindsay and Sara.

Allow God to help you use the eight strengths found in this book to make your lives everything you want them to be. The blessings are out there for you. You just have to see them, recognize them for what they are and seize the opportunity to receive them!

And to my sister, Amanda.

Thank you for always being there for me, even during the most difficult times in my life. I know our childhood wasn't always the easiest, but you and I were always a great team. I am so proud of you for all that you have accomplished in your life. May God's blessings be upon you and Todd in all that you do.

And to my late mother, Lucille Toney Luckadoo.

Without you, none of the successes in my life would have been possible. Thank you for the struggles, sacrifices and tribulations you endured to make our lives better. Thank you for taking us to church every Sunday even when there were times when it was a hardship to put gas in the car to drive us there. I know that all things are part of God's plan, even the hard things. Thank you for your high expectations of Amanda and me. Without *your* expectations, we wouldn't have had any expectations of ourselves. We miss you, and I look forward to the day when I see you again.

And to my late grandfather and grandmother, Robert Glen and Cora Toney.

Your loving hands played a huge role in raising me to be the person I am today. Your lasting memories have remained vivid in my mind over these last five decades. We miss you!

FOREWORD
Grit Matters

"*Yesterday's home runs don't win today's games.*" Babe Ruth's words were shared during our first sales meeting of the year—a reminder that each member of our leadership team needed to be in a different place next year from where we were then. *How would this be achieved?*

As a walk-on basketball player at Wake Forest, I played only fifty-nine minutes during my career. I was cut from the team twice. Physically, I was outmatched in every way, and even though my job was to be ready for the role the coach assigned me, the thought of doing this for four years was daunting. Looking back, I realize that I learned the value of showing up, the significance of continuous improvement and the fact that God's grace is sufficient for each day. Whether in basketball or business, winning matters, but producing for your team, company or family is tough, and it takes endurance to survive.

In a 2007 study at the University of Pennsylvania, psychologist Angela Duckworth looked at a variety of challenging settings for both children and adults. Her main question in each case was, "Who is successful and why?" She went to West Point military academy to see which cadets would survive training. Her team attended the National Spelling Bee to see which kids would advance to the finals. They visited schools in tough neighborhoods to see which first-year teachers would still be teaching at the end of the year. And she partnered with various companies in the private sector to see which salespeople would keep their jobs and even earn the most money.

"In all of those very different contexts, one characteristic emerged as a significant predictor of success," Duckworth says, "and it wasn't social intelligence, it wasn't good looks, physical health, and it wasn't IQ. *It was grit.* Grit is passion and perseverance for very long-term goals. It's having stamina. Grit is sticking with your future day-in day-out—not just for the week, not just for the month, but for years."

Whatever grit is, Robert Luckadoo has it. His story is a reminder that while challenge is inevitable, we don't have to be defined by our adversities. We don't have to *stop*—we can keep *going*.

I recently had a chance to play golf with Robert, and as we were riding in the cart, he shared bits and pieces of his testimony, including tough moments from his childhood that required a young man to take ownership of his life quicker than most. During all of these recollections, however, I could feel the joy and fulfillment derived from his trusting that even our trials are gifts from God. It was clear that a choice was made to press onward and never stop running the race.

> *The Gospel makes the worst times tolerable and the best times leavable.*
> —JOHN NEWTON

Through his recounting of genuine experiences and with a Gospel-centered worldview in mind, Robert outlines eight principles of leadership that reflect what it means to have *grit in your craw*. As Robert will convey, grit is not about circumstance and social position but about a certain kind of determination and toughness that doesn't always show up in the box score.

You could describe Robert Luckadoo as a renaissance man. Coach, entrepreneur, pilot, race car driver, insurance professional, husband, father—he's done it all, and he's done it all with great success! I believe he's been able to embrace new challenges not only because he *shows up* but because he is the kind of person who gets up in the morning and gives everything he has even though he doesn't necessarily know what the result will be.

Whether you're in real estate, insurance, financial services, athletics, or another performance-based position, the ensuing pages will challenge you to be the best possible version of yourself within the role that you play. This book fills a major need for anyone with production-based job requirements.

"Two roads diverged in a yellow wood and I took the road less traveled," Robert Frost wrote. On the less traveled road, Robert Luckadoo—with much humility and grace—not only encourages us to have *grit in our craw* but also points us toward the things in life that endure.

Alan Williams
Teammates Matter, author | founder
Teammatesmatter.com
Co-president, BCW Food Products

CONTENTS

Foreword		v
Eight Strengths You Can't Succeed Without		1
The Foundation		5
1	Diligence	13
2	Tenacity	23
3	Optimism	31
4	Flexibility	45
5	Discipline	57
6	Resilience	73
7	Confidence	83
8	Purpose	95
A Closing Note		107
Acknowledgments		111
About the Author		113

EIGHT STRENGTHS YOU CAN'T SUCCEED WITHOUT

I DON'T BELIEVE IN LUCK. Even though it's right there in my last name—*Luck*adoo—I just don't buy it. I don't believe in good luck, I don't believe in bad luck. What I do believe is that you can create your own good fortune through the blessings God has given you, the opportunities you've been presented with in life. He has also given us the ability to make choices, and it's up to us to see our blessings for what they are and make the most of them. With perseverance and hard work, we can use our blessings to *make* our own luck.

It's amazing how "lucky" you can be if you just make the choice to work hard and persevere. When it comes to your career, it starts with simply choosing to get up and go to work in the morning. And it continues with choosing to be productive when you get there—choosing to be a positive beacon at the office rather than spending the morning visiting with your colleagues and grumbling about something you have no control over, or hanging out at the water cooler and sharing your disdain with anyone who will listen.

And it doesn't stop there. *Everything's* a choice. Whatever your job may be, whatever career path you're on, you're always at a fork in the road. You wake up every day with a choice to make: Which direction will you go? What you are going to make of the day? You can coast through it, doing as little as possible, or you can make it *your* day and get as much out of every moment as you can. God has given you the opportunity, and now the choice is yours. What are you going to do with it?

There's an old southern expression that I think perfectly captures what it takes to succeed: "a little grit in your craw." It's a reference to the sand and pebbles that birds keep in their gizzards to help break up food, since they don't have the digestive stomach acids that humans have. So the term "a little grit in your craw" refers to qualities like courage and determination that people use to "break down" challenging situations into manageable situations—qualities that we can use to take advantage of the opportunities God gives all of us.

When we think back, it's clear that God has given us many opportunities over our lifetimes and challenged us to capitalize on them. And He's given us many talents we can use to do just that. So everything's in place—we have everything we need to be successful. But it's ultimately up to us to recognize those opportunities when they're presented to us and to maximize our talents. It's up to us to put a little grit in our craws and turn challenges into victories. Are you using your talents and taking advantage of your blessings and opportunities? Only you can answer that question. Take a few minutes to think about it.

I believe everything happens for a reason and that the blessings and opportunities we're given—or that are taken from us—are all part of God's plan for us. And I believe the hardships we're dealt are also part of God's plan for us. If you believe that, too, then luck truly doesn't have any part in our lives. Someone once asked me, "If you don't believe in luck, then how do you explain a person winning the lottery?" Well, that happened for a reason, too. That's also a part of God's plan. At the other extreme, what about a child's death from cancer? Could that really be part of God's plan? Without a doubt. I believe with all my heart that when such profound events occur, both good and bad, they are indeed part of God's plan.

I wrote this book to inspire those who believe, as I do, that God has a plan for our lives, and especially for those who believe we have to make the absolute most of that plan. As we look around at the world today, it's easy to become callous, to become frustrated with the direction we seem to be headed in as a society, as a country and as a world. But we have to remember that each of us is an important part of God's plan for the world. He has placed us here to be successful, in both our personal and professional lives, and to carry his message to the masses through our words and our actions.

My hope is that you find the eight essential strengths I cover in this book to be a road map for your success, a small prism of clarity in a world shrouded in fog. I hope you'll embrace these eight must-have qualities—diligence, tenacity, optimism, flexibility, discipline, resilience, confidence and purpose—and use them to your great advantage. God truly has a plan for your life, and by finding these qualities within yourself and making the most of them, you can and will carry out that plan.

THE FOUNDATION

> "I consider that our present sufferings are not worth comparing with the glory that will be revealed in us."
>
> —Romans 8:18

Ever met someone who was larger than life? You know the type—the life of the party, the guy everyone wants to be around because he's so interesting and his radius of influence is where all the fun is. My dad was one of those people. At least that's the way I remember him.

I recall, as a young child, climbing with my dad to a rocky peak in New Mexico to explore a cave where he claimed that Indians had hidden out to ambush a stagecoach. I remember washing back the black sand to uncover my first flakes of yellow gold as he taught me how to pan in the narrow streams of Golden Valley,

North Carolina. My dad taught me how to use a metal detector to hunt for gold in the old mining towns of the West. He took me on a journey from Fort Pierce, Florida, to Key West and back by boat. He took me deep into the Florida Everglades to hunt for panthers and alligators. And once we even climbed down into a large volcanic crater in Arizona or New Mexico to look for rattlesnake nests and found several! Definitely larger than life, my dad.

But then, suddenly, he was gone.

I remember it like it was yesterday. It was a warm, bright late-spring day in the foothills of western North Carolina, one of those days where it's just great to be alive, especially as a sixth-grader without a care in the world. It's funny how the memory works sometimes—smells, sounds and even the temperature of a particular day come alive decades later. The outfield grass on the baseball field was the deepest, darkest green, a green you see on fields in the South only in late spring. After a long winter's nap, the daffodils were in full, brilliant-yellow splendor, the trees were budding and, as my grandpa used to say, the sap was rising. I can still see the robins hopping around in right field as I stand at shortstop position. We were at recess, just after lunch, and while most of the boys were playing a pickup baseball game, the other students were hanging out on the big concrete steps along the third-base line, talking and laughing and just being kids—a typical spring scene in the life of a sixth-grader.

Just as the batter was about to step to the plate, one of my classmates sitting on the bleachers yelled, "Robert, there's your mom." I didn't think much of it at first; sometimes she came by to pick up me and my sister, Mandy, in the afternoon. But as I crouched into position to get ready for the pitch, the batter stepped out of the box and pointed to left field. When I turned around, my mother and Mandy were quickly walking toward me through that deep green outfield grass, holding hands. My mother was crying and Mandy had a look of dire fear on her face. "Oh my gosh," I thought, "what's happened to Mandy? Does she have a stomach virus?" But then I realized it couldn't be that. Judging by my mom's expression, it was much worse than a stomach virus.

As she approached me, her head fell and she began sobbing.

"He's gone, Robbie." She struggled to get the words out.

"Who's gone?" I said.

"Daddy ... He's gone." My mom's voice trembled as she looked up at me. "I am so, so sorry."

"Where did he go? Back to work in Tennessee?" Despite my attempts at denial, I realized that this was very serious.

"Robbie, your daddy had a massive heart attack last night in his hotel room in Tennessee, and he's gone."

At that moment, all the memories of my dad rushed through my head like a whirlpool, a timeline spinning out of control, and then they slowy disappeared like water down a drain and a wave of nausea began to build in my stomach. I couldn't believe this was happening to me, to my mom, to our family. A moment ago, I was a happy twelve-year-old playing ball at recess and basking in the spring sun, and suddenly my life had been changed forever. *Why me? Why Mom? Why us?*

As devasted as I was, little did I know how life-altering my dad's death would be for us. Until that moment on the afternoon of May 9, 1977, we'd been an average middle-class family. Not having finished a postsecondary education, Mom was a stay-at-home mom. My dad, who'd been in textile sales, had been the sole provider for the family. And now we had *no* provider. And not a dollar's worth of life insurance to fall back on—my dad hadn't taken out a policy.

I have no idea how my mother paid for the funeral. I'm sure some of our family pitched in, but I never had the heart to ask her how she managed it. I do know this, though: The next three years of our lives were very difficult. We didn't have enough money to stay in our home, Mom's car was repossessed, we got our clothes from Goodwill and we had to use food stamps and stand in line for government cheese. In a word, our world had been turned upside down.

You're probably wondering why I would begin an inspirational book, a book about eight character traits that can transform your career and your life, with such a tragic story. The reason is that I wanted to introduce you to my mother. If it weren't for her, I wouldn't be sitting here today at my laptop paying others forward through this book. My mom, God rest her soul, was the embodiment of the eight life-changing qualities I'm going to tell you about. At age forty-six, with two children ages eight and twelve, she went back to college to get the education she needed to make a better life for our family. While working twelve-hour shifts as a clerk at the local general store, she attended class on her days off and in the evenings until she graduated from Gardner Webb College with a bachelor's degree in education.

And she didn't stop there. Almost as soon as she got her first teaching job at the local elementary school, she enrolled in Western Carolina University's master's program for education, where she graduated with honors two years later. Then she continued her education as a postgraduate student in the WCU education administration program and became a dearly loved educator and an inspiration to hundreds of children in the Rutherford County, North Carolina, school system.

I still have her first pay stub from the Rutherford schools. Her take-home pay for that first month was $630.08 I remember how proud she was of that first check. If it had been for $10 million, she couldn't have been any prouder. We were proud of her, too.

A God-fearing Southern Baptist, my mother was, without a doubt, the strongest-willed woman I've ever known. She wouldn't accept sympathy from anyone. She was too proud for that. She never wanted anyone to be sad about her dire situation. She was a positive beacon of light in a world of despair. She had a purpose in life—to make our lives and the lives of the people around us better—and that purpose didn't allow room for the acceptance of sympathy. In a heartbeat, she'd gone from a happy-go-lucky middle-class mom to a homeless widow with no car, no income, no education, two small children, and only her strong will and her faith in God to pull us through, and that's what she did.

Mom passed away from pancreatic cancer in 2003, and like me, she believed that everything happens for a reason, that it's all part of God's plan. She had the utmost faith and trust in God—there was nothing she couldn't conquer with God's help and blessing. She believed that no matter what hand you were dealt in life, if you accepted it as part of God's plan, worked hard toward solutions and persevered through the hardships, your blessings would be great when you turned the corner on those difficulties. They would far outweigh the pain and suffering you experienced along the way. And she was right. In my own life, the blessings have been greater than the suffering every time.

For my sister and me, Mom's greatest legacy is our expectations of ourselves. Failure was never an option at our house. She expected that we would be successful and instilled the same expectation in us. To her, there was no other option than success. She raised us to persevere and be triumphant through all life's trials and tribulations, and to always focus on the blessings on the other side.

And now, although she's gone, she really isn't. The eight requisites of success that were at the very core of her makeup, like a DNA strand tucked away within every nucleus of her body and woven throughout the framework of her soul, didn't die with her. She passed them on to my sister and me through her actions, her expectations, her unconditional positive outlook and her love. And now I hope to pass them on to you.

I hope the eight qualities that are the focus of this book inspire you to become a beacon of light for those in your life. I hope they help you to meet the challenges of your life with hope and promise. And most of all, I hope they inspire you to take advantage of every opportunity that God provides you.

1 DILIGENCE

> "Lazy hands make a man poor, but diligent hands bring wealth."
> —Proverbs 10:4

> "The sluggard craves and gets nothing, but the desires of the diligent are fully satisfied."
> —Proverbs 13:4

My mother's father, Robert Glen Toney, known as RG to his friends and affectionately as Paw-Paw to us grandchildren, was a hard-working farmer from the foothills of western North Carolina. Born May 9, 1906, he'd had a tough upbringing. He grew up during the turbulent times of World War I in a little hollow tucked back in the hills near Golden Valley, North Carolina. His parents were survivors, poor in assets but rich in family. They grew and raised their own food and supplemented their diets with the native wild game they could take from the surrounding hillsides. They dipped their water from a hand-dug well or retrieved it from one of the springs in the area, and they used a privy out behind their old tin-roofed wood-board house. Each child got one pair of new shoes per year, and most of their clothes were handmade.

The RG I knew was a tough, strong-willed survivor like his parents, with calluses on his hands and a red-clay sweat stain around the rim of his hat. He rolled his cigarettes from Prince Albert in a can, dipped Tube Rose sweet snuff and spent most of his productive years in low-gallused overalls and three-quarter height Red Wing leather lace-up boots, as he followed a team of plow mules across the cotton fields of Rutherford County. For all his outward strength and his hardened image, though, he had a huge heart. With the passing of my dad early in my life, he and my grandmother more or less adopted me as one of their own. A large part of who I am today, I owe to RG and Cora Toney.

I spent many days in my early childhood walking behind my grandfather's plow in the newly turned rows of North Carolina clay. That was in the days before NAFTA and the shipment of many of our county's jobs to Mexico, when cotton was the lifeblood of the area and the fields covered the rolling foothills of the region. Farmers planted it, tended it and harvested it. The cotton gins that dotted the landscape employed local citizens to gin the seeds out of the fluffy white bolls, and thousands of other Rutherford County residents worked in the mills' spinning, weaving, dyeing and jacquard plants. Many of the country's largest textile corporations called western North Carolina home.

Cotton is a labor-intensive crop to produce. In late fall and early winter, the fields must be turned over with a plow to rejuvenate the soil and rid the upper layer of any weeds that have taken root after harvest. In preparation for planting the cotton seeds, the fields must be harrowed with discs to loosen the clods and smooth out the soil for the delicate seeds. In late spring, after the last frost, the cotton seeds are planted in long straight rows, and as the seeds sprout and take growth in early summer, the rows are again plowed to save the seedlings from the onslaught of morning glories, crab grass and kudzu along the edges of the field. Throughout the summer, the mature cotton plants are laid by—more or less left alone because they can now fend for themselves—while thousands of bees and other insects pollinate the beautiful yellow blooms. Finally, by early October, those once-brilliant green stems and yellow blooms have been transformed into the woody hues of fall. The stems have traded their heavy green foliage for endless bolls of fluffy snow-white cotton that have proudly burst open in the cool autumn air.

For the cotton farmer, whose income was directly proportionate to how many of those big, fluffy bolls of cotton he had at the end of the season, a lot of blood, sweat and time spent behind that mule team stood between the turning, harrowing and preparation of the field in early spring, and the picking of the crop in October. My grandfather and his mules had to cover every row of his fields four times a season, not counting the picking and bailing. He had to disc it, lay it off and plant it, and plow it after it became established, and after the picking was complete, he had to turn the ground over. All these years later, I've still seen no greater example of diligence than my Paw-Paw and those mules.

A typical day in their lives went something like this: My grandfather lines the mules up at the end of a half-mile row, yells "Heee-yah" and pops the reins. As the mules start pulling toward the short-range goal—the other end of the field—the plow starts to sink into the clay. Along the way to the other end, though, there are lots of distractions that can knock them off their course. For example, there are big rocks in the field—what's left of the granite from which the clay formed over eons—and those rocks can toss the plow right out of the ground. Imagine being forced out of furrow after furrow and having to stop and get realigned every time. But thanks to the leather blinders the mules are fitted with—blinding them to everything but the other end of the field—they never lose their focus on the short-range goal and they get right back to work. Diligently, they drag the plows through the rocky ground, exposing the turned soil to the light of day and filling the air with its earthy, invigorating scent.

When summer arrives, so does another distraction: big, green, nasty horseflies that attack animals and people alike. Their bite can feel like a shot from a ten-gauge hypodermic needle, and when they let go, they even leave a little trickle of blood behind. To ward them off, the mules keep their tails in constant motion, but occasionally one gets past their defenses. Horseflies are no match for mules when it comes to diligence, though. Even painful bites don't distract mules from their goal.

And neither does the Carolinas' brutal summertime heat, which can exceed 100 in the afternoon, and that's on top of humidity of 90 percent or more. In these conditions, those black mules get so hot that their coats lather under the harnesses and the bits in their mouths drip with foamy saliva. But they're diligent—even though it might as well be a summer day in the Sahara without a shade tree in sight, they push on, never losing sight of their goal.

And finally, after enduring a half-mile's worth of rocky ground, biting flies and merciless heat, they reach that goal— the other end of the field. But what do they do *then*? Do they take a much-deserved break? Knock off for the day? No, they do an about-face and immediately set their sights on the *next* goal, which is actually the same as the last goal: the other end of the field. As long as there's a furrow to plow between them and the other end of the field, that's what they'll be doing. Now *that's* diligence.

If this story were set in the corporate world, my grandfather would be the upper-level manager of the bunch. He'd be the strategic planner, the brains behind the operation. He'd be privy to and constantly aware of both the short- and long-range goals. But he'd also play a hands-on role in the achievement of those goals—he'd line up his team, yell "Heee-yah" and pop the reins. He'd also be there to offer encouragement, help the team push past distractions and make subtle changes or corrections as necessary along the way.

On the farm, my grandfather had midrange goals, like finishing the final row before dark, and long-range strategic goals, like harvesting the cotton at the end of the season. But he was also very much a member of the team in the field. For every step the mules took, he probably took three to keep up. He held them accountable for their actions and didn't manage them from a distance. He kept them focused on the other end of the field, never letting distractions—the rocks, the horseflies, the sweltering sun—steer them off course. And at the end of the day, he brushed them, fed and watered them and praised them for a job well-done.

All the while, my grandfather diligently kept his eye on the goals for his team and his family. Sound like a manager you'd want to work for? Sound like a manager you'd want to *be*?

Looking at the three main characters of this story—my grandfather, his team of mules and the plow—which one do you see yourself as? It's always nice to be my grandfather—the top guy—but you have to spend some time in the trenches first, and I'm sure we've all been mules at one time or another in our careers. We've carried the loads of our managers and our teams on our backs, and we've remained focused on the short-term goal, ever mindful of keeping our rows straight and not letting the distractions of life at the office get to us.

And life at the office certainly comes with its share of rocks, horseflies and sweltering heat! For instance, we can be sitting at our desk fully absorbed in the task at hand—we can be *gettin' it done*, with productivity beaming from every ounce of our being—and then *bam*, the phone rings.

You pick it up. "It's Mrs. Bradbury on line two," your receptionist says.

Silence.

A wave of nausea starts at your toes, rolls through your gut and crashes against your frontal lobe, where it transforms into the beginnings of a tension headache. Mrs. Bradbury is one of your top customers but also one of the most annoying, and she's calling to find out why the insurance premium on her 8,500-square-foot waterfront home went up eighty-four dollars this year. And, like she also does every Monday at this time, she'll tell you she went over her policy from cover to cover over the weekend, and she'll want to go over the coverages for the 187 items of jewelry and artwork on her inland marine policy.

"And by the way, could you give me a quote for full coverage on a 2015 Mercedes SUV? I'm thinking about trading in my Porsche Cayenne," she says proudly, an hour and nineteen minutes into your weekly conversation.

Sound familiar? I bet you've dealt with clients like this in your business, too. They're like the rocks and the horseflies on the farm, doing their best to distract us from our goal—the other end of the field. No matter what line of work you're in, if it's production-based—if you get paid in direct proportion to what you produce on a daily basis—these little distractions can move you off target and waste big chunks of your day. But we need to exercise diligence. We need to keep the goal in sight. Yes, you may have been in the middle of a very productive exercise when Mrs. Bradbury called, but ultimately we can't let a relatively minor distraction like that cause us to lose sight of our goal. And that's where our ability to choose comes in. We can *choose* whether to allow distractions to scramble our focus and bring our work to a crashing halt. Diligence is the key! We have to remain diligent in the pursuit of our goals, no matter the size of the rocks or the horseflies.

And then there's the plow. In my life, I've been the plow many times, and I'm sure you have, too. The plow is the guy in the trenches with the roll-up-your-sleeves, down-and-dirty, "git 'er done" attitude who's doing just that—gittin' 'er done. Sure, your hard work is underappreciated, but you don't need praise. And sometimes being the plow isn't so bad. After all, when you're dug in and working hard, it's easy to minimize the distractions. If you have the willpower, you can just swat those horseflies or kick those rocks right out of the way and keep on digging.

As the plow, you never even look up to see the other end of the field, and that's not so bad either. Your midlevel and upper management—the mules and the farmer—will take care of the goals. Occasionally, they'll reset the goal and turn you in a different direction—toward the other end of the field—but once again, diligence carries the day. Rocks don't bother you. A change in direction doesn't bother you. You rely on the farmer and the mules to guide you in the right direction, to make sure you're in line, to help you when you hit the occasional rock and, at the end of the day, to let you cool off a little after a job well-done. No praise necessary. Fittingly, you have the resolve of steel: "Just drop me in the ground, point me in the right direction and get out of my way."

Whatever role you're playing in your career at the moment—the farmer, the mules or the plow—you need to work in unison with others if the team's going to achieve its goals.

The farmer needs to put together a plan to best utilize the resources he has available. He's assembled what he believes to be the best possible team of mules and harnessed them to the best plow on the market, and now he has to move them to action to achieve the team's goals. And he has to do it by *leading*. Mules are stubborn animals and can't be pushed—they have to be led. And I'm not talking about walking in front of them and pulling and dragging them back and forth across a hundred-acre field. They have to be led from the rear through trust and assurance and confidence that their leader knows what's best for them and has made them part of the team. They need a guiding force to set them in motion toward a common goal.

And when the plow hits a rock, or the horseflies start biting, or the heat becomes oppressive, the team members must keep their eyes on the short-range goal—the other end of the field—because that's how *long*-range goals are met. One row at a time. When the crop is harvested at the end of the season, all that diligence and hard work will have been worth it.

In your life, be diligent, just as my grandfather and his mules were, because as Proverbs says, "the soul of the diligent is richly supplied."

2 TENACITY

"Therefore, since we are surrounded by such a great cloud of witnesses, let us throw off everything that hinders and the sin that so easily entangles, and let us run with perseverance the race that is marked out for us."

—Hebrews 12:1

"Consider it pure joy, my brothers, whenever you face trials of many kinds, because you know that the testing of your faith develops perseverance. Perseverance must finish its work so that you may be mature and complete, not lacking anything."

—James 1:2-4

As a young boy in rural western North Carolina, I couldn't wait to get out of school for the summer. I remember sitting in class on those warm May days, with the laser-like sunbeams streaking through the open paned windows onto the old pine-wood floors of the schoolhouse. The smell of freshly cut fescue grass mingled perfectly with that distinctive varnish scent of an old school building that's been tightly sealed for the winter, but now stretches its girders in the warm late-spring sun—a scent I could almost taste. From the third-floor classroom we could hear a lawnmower running in the distance and students playing on the playground. We strained to concentrate on the lesson being taught but paid more attention to the big clock over the door, praying the three o'clock bell would ring just a minute early. It was only a few days until summer vacation, and all I could think about was freedom.

The thoughts of my childhood summers still bring a warmth to my heart and an energizing feeling to my soul. They were spent at my grandparents' farm, where they lived in a quaint red brick house nestled in a grove of mature oaks just east of a little town called Ellenboro. The winding, single-lane gravel road took you about a mile from the asphalt pavement of State Highway 74 to their home. I still get a little giddy when I recall the carefree feeling I always had as my mom turned the last corner into the heart of that stand of shade oaks, knowing my summer haven was only minutes away. I can still vividly see the old beige Ford Maverick parked in the carport, my grandma and grandpa in their rocking chairs on the front porch stringing beans or shucking corn.

As much as I loved it, passing the time on the farm on those long sultry summer days could be a challenge. We're talking about the time from the late '60s to the late '70s. There were no computers, no iPads, iPods, iPhones or PlayStations. We had rocks, sticks, dirt, acorns, hickory nuts, the little grassy plants that have spears for seeds, a few matchbox cars, a GI Joe and some little plastic toy soldiers. If we were lucky, sometimes my uncle would buy a few firecrackers around the Fourth of July.

There wasn't even a color TV. In fact, I don't even remember having a color TV until I was in high school. We did have a remote control, though—*I* was the remote. "Turn it over to Channel 3. Walter Cronkite is getting ready to come on," Paw-Paw would say, and I'd get up and turn it to Channel 3 with the big round clicker knob on the front of the set. Besides Channel 3, the CBS affiliate out of Charlotte, we had Channel 9, the NBC station out of Charlotte, and Channel 13, the ABC station from Asheville. How many more channels could you need? We had a high-definition picture, too—after I adjusted the rabbit-ear antennas, stood on one leg, moved the piece of tin foil connected to them to another location on the wall and slightly adjusted the tuner with a plastic disc just behind the big dial that changed the channels. Once I did all that, the black-and-white image of Walter would come in just clearly enough to be seen through all the snow on the screen.

It took a lot of tenacity—or perseverance, as the Bible refers to it—to perfectly adjust that picture, but I had nothing on the tenacity of the ants in my grandparents' yard. Down South, ant species are as plentiful as the heat. There are carpenter ants, a medium-size brownish ant that can get into the walls of your house and destroy your wood framing just like termites can. There are fire ants, which come in all sizes and colors and are very aggressive. They live in a cavernous underground ant metropolis and can lay a stinging on you that a scorpion would be proud of, and one you won't soon forget. In fact, you won't forget it for months, because that's how long you'll be scratching it after the fester and redness are long gone.

And then there are tiny "pissants," barely large enough to see. If you leave a Fig Newton or a peppermint stick or anything else that's sweet on the kitchen counter, they'll break it up and tenaciously carry every last morsel back to their nest in your kitchen walls or floor. They move in perfect unison from their lair to the sweet deliciousness on the countertop, and then back home in a straight, perfectly orchestrated line. And if you mash them, the horrendous, pungent odor of their juices will be on your fingers all day, no matter how much soap you use. Not exactly what you'd expect from creatures with a diet so high in sugar.

But out in my grandparents' yard was the most tenacious of all the ants, the most evil and most dastardly: black ants. They're big and fast and have huge pincers, and they lived in colonies all across my grandparents' yard. The entrances to their underground domains were marked by mounds of freshly excavated sand, and they made little trails that led from one anthill to another like the lines on a road map. Throughout the day, they would peek out of those little entrances with their evil black eyes as if to say "Na-na-na-na-na, you can't catch me."

As a seven-year-old, I declared war on those big black ants and spent entire days, from sunup to sunset, battling them (I told you passing the time could be a challenge). I would set up my troops of plastic army men on the front lines next to the big ant colonies, I'd bring GI Joe and his buddies in from the rear flank in a Jeep, and we'd wage an aerial assault on the front lines with rocks and sticks. Then I'd take up a sniper's position with my BB gun and pick off the survivors.

By the end of the day, the anthills looked as if they'd been ravaged by an *actual* war. They'd been blasted with firecrackers, dug out with sticks and my grandmother's trowel, stomped with GI Joe shoes, run over with matchbox cars, shot repeatedly with BBs, hammered by slingshots and soaked with bottles of water. Yet when I would step outside to survey the battlefields the next morning, the anthills looked pristine again, as if none of it had ever happened.

Looking back on those battles, I realize that in the years since, I've never seen anything as tenacious as those big black ants. Imagine how hard they had to work every night to restore their colony to pristine condition so that they were ready for the next day's work, battles and all. You truly couldn't tell that their home had been decimated less than twenty-four hours before. The battlefield was clear, their house was in order and they were prepared for whatever the day would bring. Imagine the tenacity it took to stand their ground every day.

Do you demonstrate the same tenacity in your own battles? Do you clear your battlefield—and your desk—of the day's debris every night so that you can start fresh the next day? Or does your battlefield look the same today as it did yesterday and even the day before? As a performance-based professional—whether you're a project manager, a sales manager, a corporate manager, a small-business owner or an entrepreneur—you have to be tenacious, just like those black ants. You have to clear your head of the previous day's battles and march right back into action every morning. You have to have a little grit in your craw, as you take on the daily challenges of your profession.

As humans, we're tempted to carry grudges, to let little things bother us for days on end. Sometimes the smallest, most unimportant things get under our skin like a burr under a horse's saddle. These nagging irritations eat at us and eat at us, sapping us of any semblance of productivity.

But professionals whose livelihoods are reliant on what they produce every day can't allow a battle that was lost yesterday to affect the productivity needed today.

We have to be tenacious. We're not going to win every battle—that's just life. We have to let go of the nagging little battles, most of which we have no control over, that are robbing us of our productivity. Sometimes the little army of plastic soldiers is going to surround us and GI Joe is going to plant his boots right across our anthill. But just like the ants, we can't carry that loss to the next battleground. We can't hold on to it till the next day, or even the next client. We have to constantly clear our battlefields, just like the ants did. As professionals, we need to focus on the things that are important *now*. We can't allow the big case we'd been working on for months but lost to a competitor dictate how we apply ourselves to the three cases we still have. If we carry the negativity of the lost battle into the front lines of the other three cases, chances are we'll find a way to lose those, too.

"Only worry about the things that you can control," a great manager once told me. "The other things will take care of themselves." How true that statement has proved to be over the years. Those ants couldn't control a bored seven-year-old kid's daily attack on their colony, but they *could* control how they reacted to it. Every morning they restored the battlefield and started with a clean slate. They didn't let yesterday's losses affect today's potential successes.

It may seem like a superficial comparison, but if you give it some thought, it actually runs pretty deep. Performance-based professionals really do have to have the tenacity of a big black ant. You can't allow lost battles to affect your approach to new challenges. You have to clean your slate—not to mention your desk—after each battle. Even if the pressures of battling GI Joe, a platoon of plastic soldiers and a fleet of matchbox cars are a daily reality for you, remain tenacious just like the ants. Keep your head clear, your attitude positive and your focus sharp as you forge ahead. Get up the next morning ready to sell that next client, achieve your next goal, and win your next battle.

3 OPTIMISM

"Have I not commanded you? Be strong and courageous. Do not be terrified; do not be discouraged, for the Lord your God is with you wherever you go."

—Joshua 1:9

"Do not let any unwholesome talk come out of your mouths, but only what is helpful for building others up according to their needs, that it may benefit those who listen."

—Ephesians 4:29

"May the God of hope fill you with all joy and peace as you trust in him, so that you may overflow with hope by the power of the Holy Spirit."

—Romans 15:13

When I arrived on the Raleigh campus of North Carolina State University as a freshman pre-med major in 1983, the whole city was still abuzz about the NCAA basketball championship. There were signs and banners all over campus bearing accolades for coach Jim Valvano and the Wolfpack, who had been victorious in the final game against the Houston Cougars just a few months before. Valvano and his staff had become overnight legends in Raleigh and across the Atlantic Coast Conference region. Coach V had led a team of young, unheralded, virtually unknown basketball players to an achievement that almost no one in college basketball could have predicted.

They'd won the ACC championship to get into the NCAA tournament and then managed to eke out five close wins and earn the nickname "the Cardiac Pack" on their way to the championship game against a powerful Houston squad. It was a true David-and-Goliath matchup, with none of the oddsmakers giving Valvano's Wolfpack even a chance to stay in the game against Houston's well-known, highly talented "Phi Slamma Jamma" team of human highlight reels. But in the end, Lorenzo Charles's dunk at the buzzer gave the team the championship and put Valvano and his Cardiac Pack in basketball's hall of immortality.

Afterward, thousands of students and fans rushed onto Hillsborough Street, the northern boundary of the NC State campus. Huge bonfires were lighted and the party went on for days. Even when I arrived to move into my dorm five months later, there was still toilet paper in the trees, burn scars in the asphalt on Hillsborough Street, and a certain madness among the student body. I'd attended several games that season and couldn't wait until the next one. I was officially a Wolfpacker now.

A few weeks into the semester, I was sitting at my cramped little dorm-room desk, with a dim lamp lighting my biology notes from the past three weeks. I was studying for my first big college exam, scheduled for 7:50 the following morning. I'd left the comfort of my little hometown in the foothills of western North Carolina to take on the challenges of attending one of the state's largest public universities, and I was a little nervous about the test, especially given the amount of material that would be covered. But I was a pretty good student and knew that with enough preparation, I would do just fine.

It was September and still very, very hot, and back in 1983, most dorms didn't have air conditioning, including mine. The hum of the little oscillating window fan had nearly put me into a trance as it alternately flipped the pages of my biology notes on one side of the room and my roommate's calculus notes on the other side. But suddenly the ringing of the dorm-suite phone in the hallway brought me back to full attention. I heard one of my suite mates answer it on the second ring.

"Hello? … Robert? Yes."

I started for the door, and my biology notes blew all over my side of the room.

"Yes, I think he's in. Could you hold for just a second please?" There was a knock at the door. "Robert, the phone is for you."

Expecting the call to be from my mom, I answered with a casual "Hello?"

"Hello, Robert, this is Jim Valvano. How are you this evening?"

Dead silence as I attempted to catch my lower jaw before it could hit the tile floor. I knew that either it really was Jim Valvano or it was a recording of him, because he had a very distinctive raspy voice. A thousand thoughts ran through my head. Which one of my college buddies had played this prank on me?

"Hello? Are you there?"

I hadn't been able to muster a single word. Think about it—I was just an eighteen-year-old kid from a tiny town in western North Carolina studying for a biology test and, out of the blue, basketball legend Jim Valvano calls me in my dorm. Something just wasn't right with this picture.

"Uh ... yes, sir, Mr. Valvano. Uh, doing fine, sir, just studying for a biology test, sir." I just knew I was going to hear my best friend, Gary, horse laughing at me on the other end of the line at any second. I figured I'd play along with the prank, though.

Optimism | 35

"That's great, Robert. I was talking with your Uncle John this week, and he was telling me how much of a basketball fan you are and how much you like the NC State Wolfpack," Valvano said in a polite, very businesslike fashion.

It *was* him. None of my friends knew my uncle was coaching basketball at Salem (Virginia) High School, where he had a superstar junior guard/forward named Richard Morgan. One of the best players in Virginia and maybe even the top recruit in the Southeast, Morgan was being recruited nationally by every large basketball program, including the Wolfpack.

"Robert, the coaches and I have been talking, and we would like for you to consider being our manager for the Wolfpack basketball team this year. Would something like that be of interest to you?"

Are you kidding me? Did he really just say what I think he just said? "Uh … yes, sir … uh, Jim, uh, Mr. V, uh, Coach, uh, Valvano. That would be great, sir!" It was like my brain was turning so fast that my mouth couldn't keep up with it.

"Well, that's great!" Coach Valvano said. "How about coming down to my office at Case Athletics Center tomorrow after class to meet with me and the coaching staff. I'll introduce you to my assistants and we can discuss the position." I couldn't believe what I was hearing. "Once we talk tomorrow, you can let us know then if it's something you would be interested in. Would 2 p.m. work for you tomorrow?"

I took a deep breath and thought about my schedule. "Yes, sir, coach. I get out of class at one and will see you at 2 p.m."

"Great! And good luck on that biology test!"

I hung up the phone, went back into my room and sat on the bed in total disbelief.

"Who was that?" my roommate said. Judging by his face, I must have been as pale as a ghost.

"It was just Jim Valvano," I said, finally mustering a smile.

Needless to say, we didn't get a lot of studying done for the rest of the evening. Instead, my suite mates and I discussed my call from Jimmy V well into the night. It turned out that the suite mate who'd answered the phone had recognized Coach Valvano's voice and alerted the others, and they'd all listened to the conversation through their doors. After we finally called it a night, I tossed and turned in my little dorm bed, playing the conversation with Coach Valvano over in my head a million times. Had I really been on the phone with *the* Jim Valvano? Would I really be meeting him in just a few short hours? Disbelief swirled in my mind as I drifted off to sleep.

After acing my biology test the next morning despite my abbreviated study session, I had a quick sandwich and headed from the student center to the Case Athletic

Center. My mind raced with thoughts of the ACC tournament, the Sweet 16, the Final Four and the national championship game. I had visions of myself sitting at the end of the bench this season in a red sport jacket and a bright red tie. My pace quickened as I saw the roof of the Case center next to Reynolds Coliseum—home of the now-world-famous NC State Wolfpack.

I can't believe it. I'm getting ready to meet Jim Valvano.

At the time, the Case was the location of most of the Wolfpack coaches' offices. The athletic director's office was there, too, and so were the offices of the other highest-ranking members of the NC State athletic department. I'd passed the building in awe many times but had never ventured inside, assuming it was off limits to the general public. And now, with the recent national championship, it had taken on the air of a shrine. I pulled back one of the big glass double doors at the entrance and stepped into the foyer. The A/C-chilled air immediately invigorated me after the walk across campus in the sweltering heat. I took a deep breath, filling my lungs with as much of the championship air in this hallowed building as they could hold. My skin tingled with excitement, and I made my way to the staircase that led to the second-floor offices.

When I reached the top of the stairs, I made a right toward Coach Valvano's office, where the door was wide open. Sitting at his desk, with the huge national championship trophy sitting on a corner of it, he looked just like he did on TV.

He'd seen me coming down the hall and was almost to the door by the time I stepped in.

"Robert, I'm Jim Valvano. Very nice to meet you," Coach V said, in that familiar raspy voice, and shook my hand firmly.

Am I dreaming? Can someone please pinch me?

"Robert, I'd like for you to meet my assistant coaches. This is Tom Abatemarco. And Ed McClean."

I'm sure my palms were sweating heavily as I shook hands with these coaches whose faces had become so familiar during the television coverage of the Pack's championship run.

"Have a seat, Robert," Coach Valvano said. "We'd like to talk with you about this manager's position." He closed the door and sat in the big red leather chair behind his desk.

I couldn't take my eyes off the towering trophy.

"Robert, as you know, we are recruiting one of your uncle's top players there in Salem, Richard Morgan. Your Uncle John mentioned to me last week that you were here on campus as a freshman, and we thought it might be nice to have you come aboard as a manager for our team this year."

It all seemed surreal—the meeting, the telephone call the night before, my first big biology test, all of it happening at once. It was a bit much for an eighteen-year-old from Ellenboro, North Carolina.

We talked for about ten minutes, fifteen at the most, the three of them asking questions about my family, Ellenboro and my major and telling me about the manager's position, before Coach Valvano stood up and extended his hand.

"Sounds great! We'll be working out at Carmichael Gym tomorrow afternoon at three. Plan to be there at two to help get practice set up."

I shook his hand, thanked the coaches for their offer and headed back down the stairs toward the exit.

As I walked back to my dorm room, excitement, anxiety and fear took turns in my head. I was excited about the opportunity. How many freshmen in the entire country get a personal call in their dorm from an NCAA-champion basketball coach offering them a position on the team? I was anxious about what to expect tomorrow in my first practice with the team. And as for the fear, I was a pre-med major—I had classes in the afternoons and was taking a full load of eighteen hours as a first-semester freshman. How would I ever balance my new position with my studies?

I knew deep down that my grades and my education should be my main focus. It was important to get off to a strong start as a freshman. When I got back to my dorm, I called my mom, who was very calm in most situations and always wise. I really needed some advice on this one.

Over the course of a lengthy conversation, we discussed the pros and cons of my managerial opportunity, and we decided I should give it a try. But we also agreed that the moment it started to hamper my grades or class work, I'd step down because to get into med school, my grades were all-important. And so it was settled.

The next day's practice was awesome. The players were *huge*. To me they looked literally larger than life. And they were all very nice and welcoming to a nervous 5'11" country boy from the hills of western North Carolina. At the end of practice, I received my assignments for the upcoming week, which included assisting with the team's laundry, setting up practice every day and making sure all the equipment was put away at the end of practice.

Each manager was also assigned two players to keep tabs on to make sure they were going to class every day. My players were Lorenzo Charles and Cozelle McQueen, who shared a room in the athletes' dorm, a former motel across Western Boulevard from campus. I vividly recall the first day I sat on one of their beds while they got ready for class and noticed Lorenzo's pink fur coat hanging in the closet. I didn't know where he'd gotten it, but I'd certainly never seen an animal with pink fur in the North Carolina mountains.

As I made sure these men who towered over me had their books and assignments and walked them to their classes, it all felt more surreal than ever.

Unfortunately, I wasn't able to change my schedule to accommodate my basketball duties, because by the time I was offered the job, the drop/add/change period had passed. And after a couple of weeks, I'd missed several important classes and had made poor scores on several quizzes. Yes, I was having fun and was definitely the big man on campus as far as my friends and suite mates were concerned, but in the end, I knew I wasn't going to make a living as a basketball manager, and my grades were too important to sacrifice.

After another week, I went to Coach Valvano's office to give him and Coach Abatemarco the news that I couldn't continue as a manager. This time I wasn't scared—I knew these guys now. They'd become close acquaintances, almost friends even. Though maybe a little disappointed, they weren't upset about my decision. I think they knew in their hearts that I was making the right decision, just like I knew it despite how hard it was.

I finished the semester with a 3.8 GPA, and I found myself sitting in a floor seat, right behind the team bench, for quite a few of the Wolfpack home games that year. It was the best of both worlds.

Though my time with the team was short-lived, I'm eternally grateful to Jim Valvano for the opportunity. He was one of the most optimistic people I've ever known, and my three weeks with his organization were one of the most inspiring experiences of my life. And somehow, he was more optimistic than ever after he was diagnosed with a very aggressive form of bone cancer just a few years later.

During his battle with this terrible disease, he said something that still gives me chills: "Don't give up … Don't ever give up." And his inspirational final speech, delivered during the 1993 ESPY Awards, was even more moving. "I've just got one last thing," he said in closing. "I urge all of you, all of you, to enjoy your life, the precious moments you have. To spend each day with some laughter, and some thought to get your emotions going. To be enthusiastic every day. As Ralph Waldo Emerson once said, 'Nothing great could be accomplished without enthusiasm.' To keep your dreams alive in spite of problems, whatever you have. The ability to be able to work hard for your dreams to come true, to become a reality."

A few weeks later, Coach Valvano passed away at age 47. Before he died, though, he and ESPN formed the V Foundation for Cancer Research, and more than two decades later, it continues to live Jim's message by working toward a cure for cancer through research grants.

As performance-based professionals, we all need to watch Jim Valvano's 1993 ESPY speech from time to time. The eternal optimism evident in his words was the fire that had burned inside the hearts, minds and souls of that 1983 NCAA-champion basketball team. The team that, against all odds, found ways to overcome deficits, eke out unbelievable wins, and somehow prevail against stronger opponents. So much of what Jim said in that speech can be applied to the sales profession and to our careers as managers. You can pull off virtually any feat with an optimistic, enthusiastic, energetic attitude.

People want to buy from someone who's excited about what he's selling. People want to be led by someone who's excited about his mission and excited about leading.

Carry your vision with great pride and enthusiasm. Go into every day with an optimistic outlook, and always check your troubles at the door to your office. And most important, when you're out on sales appointments or dealing with your staff, bring lots of energy with you.

Not every appointment is going to work out the way you'd planned. Not every encounter with a client or an employee is going to be a positive one. But as the leader, as the agent, as the sales person, you have some control over the situation. You have the power to make the best of the situation. Turn the part you can control into something positive!

Within your office, your company and your life, there are always going to be people who thrive on misery. You know who I'm talking about—those naysayers who see the worst-case scenario in every situation and drag you right into the middle of it. I bet you can name a few without having to think very hard. They're the ones with the perpetual scowls on their faces. They're the ones who have a smirk or a negative comment for everything. They're the "time sucks" who plop down in your office first thing every morning and try to convince you how bad the company is, how awful your supervisors are and how life generally stinks. Have somebody in mind yet?

Well, don't get pulled into that cesspool of misery. Run as far as you can. These negative people are like human quicksand. If you dip your toe into the mire, you might be lost forever. If you spend time with these pessimistic drama-lovers, their misery will creep into your own life. It's *your* career, *your* family's livelihood, *your* life. Don't let these negative people convince you that your life is any less spectacular than it is.

Make a point to be a source of positive energy at your office every day. Let eternal optimism be your driving force. Let your light shine as a positive beacon for your product, your office and your company. Be a role model, a supporter, and a cheerleader for a colleague, and try to find a role model in your industry who can support *you*. Even the most positive people sometimes need support.

You'll be amazed to see how success follows from optimism and a positive attitude. When you're positive and optimistic, your colleagues will notice, your supervisors will notice and your clients will notice.

Coach Valvano definitely had a little grit in his craw. His immortal words say it all: "Don't give up … Don't ever give up."

4 FLEXIBILITY

> "And we know that in all things God works for the good of those who love him, who have been called according to his purpose."
> —ROMANS 8:28

AT THE END OF MY freshman year, my grades were excellent, I'd made the dean's list both semesters and I was well on my way to receiving an acceptance letter from a top medical school. Then in the fall semester of my sophomore year, I chose an elective science class called Historical Geology, and the rest is history. I had an excellent professor, Dr. Bill Showers, who brought to life the eons that our planet had seen and left me fascinated and with a strong desire for knowledge of the ways of our planet. I was mesmerized by the fossil-collecting field trips to the phosphate mines of eastern North Carolina and to the sand dunes near the beach.

By the end of the semester, I was calling Mom to discuss a potential change of major. She was a little skeptical at first.

"If you major in geology, where will you ever get a job?" she'd say.

It was a hard decision and one I prayed about many nights—my small town in the hills of western North Carolina needed far more doctors than geologists. But I felt a calling to go in the direction of geology nonetheless. And once I'd made up my mind and made the change of major official with the university, I had no regrets and never looked back. And my mother stood by me 100 percent.

I spent much of the next two and a half years working in Dr. Showers's geochemistry lab in the basement of Withers Hall, but as the time to make a decision about my long-term plans drew near, more of my time was taken up by interviews at career fairs. NC State was a top engineering school, and most engineering/geological corporations sent scouts. At the time, oil prices were moving steadily upward and many of the oil companies were expanding their exploration projects across the world.

One of the firms I interviewed with was a large oil-field service company called Schlumberger, and the interview had gone very well. But several weeks went by and I didn't hear back. My December graduation was fast approaching (my change of major had meant an extra semester of schooling), and I'd already started to clean out my Raleigh apartment in anticipation of the move to wherever my career would take me.

The week before Thanksgiving, as I was packing for the holiday break, when I planned to spend some much-needed family time, eat a lot and watch my Cowboys play football on Thanksgiving Day, the phone rang. It was the representative from Schlumberger I'd spoken with a few weeks before.

"Robert, we're very interested in hiring you and we'd like for you to come for a second interview," he said. "Would you be interested in doing that?"

It looked as if my change from pre-med to geology was getting ready to pay off! "Yes, sir. I would very much like the opportunity to talk with you again," I replied.

"Great! I thought you'd say yes, so I've taken the liberty of booking a plane ticket for you for the interview."

I'd figured the interview would be on campus or at Schlumberger's Raleigh office and was a little surprised that I'd need to fly somewhere for it. I'd never flown by myself. "OK, that sounds good," I said.

"Great then! We want you to participate in an on-the-job training interview. You'll be riding along with a Schlumberger engineer who's based out of Morgan City, Louisiana. Your flight leaves this Sunday morning from Raleigh-Durham Airport. One of our representatives will pick you up at the New Orleans airport for transport to Morgan City."

Wow, had my Thanksgiving plans ever changed. But hey, you have to be flexible.

At the crack of dawn the following Monday, the engineer I was scheduled to job-shadow and his partner picked me up at my hotel. I'd been instructed not to unpack my clothes at the hotel but to bring them with me for the shadowing session, and having no idea what to expect, I'd packed blue jeans, work boots, flannel shirts and my basic necessities in a small duffel bag. In the car, the engineer, who I'll call John, filled me in on the details of the trip.

"We'll be meeting the helicopter at the pad in thirty minutes. We have to go by the shop to pick up our testing gear to take with us on the chopper."

Helicopter? What helicopter? I didn't agree to get on a helicopter.

"The rig we're flying out to is out on the continental shelf, about 145 miles off shore." You couldn't miss the excitement in John's voice.

"Wow! Really?" I exclaimed. "How long do you think we'll be out there?" By this time, I'd figured out that getting home for Thanksgiving was no longer an option.

"We should be back in a week, I'd say. Yeah, probably by Saturday or Sunday. This particular rig is drilling more than twelve thousand feet down. It will take them three days to get the drill pipe out before we can run our tests in the hole."

I didn't even know how to respond. I hadn't expected to have to be *this* flexible.

I boarded the helicopter with John and his assistant, "Randy," at the pad at 9 a.m. sharp for the ride out to the offshore oil rig. I'd never flown in anything without wings before and had a case of nerves as I snugged down the shoulder harness and latched the chopper door to my right. Since I was their guest, they let me sit next to the pilot, and within fifteen minutes we'd left the marshes and bayous of the Mississippi Delta behind us and were over the open waters of the Gulf of Mexico. We weren't flying very high above the water, probably five hundred feet at the most, but it was high enough to see oil rigs peppered across the Gulf. They reminded me of those black-ant hills in my grandfather's backyard, and I found myself missing home, especially the Thanksgiving dinner I wouldn't be having.

About an hour and fifteen minutes into the flight, the pilot announced that we were thirty miles from our destination. His directions to us were very clear.

"Most helicopter accidents occur during landings and takeoffs. Gusts out here can blow a chopper right off the rig and into the water." He was serious! "When I touch down on the heli-pad, be ready to get out. As soon as I hear your door slam, I'm gone." He pointed to our rig, which was coming into view on the horizon. The water out there was a deep Baltic blue, and the rigs fewer and farther between.

After a safe landing on the heli-pad and an expedient disembarking from the chopper, I watched as my lifeline to civilization lifted above my head, made a 180-degree turn back to the north and disappeared out of sight across the deep blue hues of the Gulf.

We gathered our belongings from the pad and made our way down several sets of stairs to our sleeping quarters, which were located on a deck about 250 feet above the surface of the water, a little above the midway point of the rig's platform. The bunk area looked like a supersized blue Port-a-John that had been flipped onto its side and strapped to the rig. We opened the plastic door and stepped inside. There were two sets of bunk beds, one on either side of the room and strapped to the plastic walls just like the huge Port-a-John was strapped to the rig. There was a small desk with a chair and a lamp at the back wall, between the two sets of beds.

Obviously, John and Randy had slept in these beds many times, as they weren't even fazed by the quaint abode. I threw my duffel bag onto the top bunk and climbed up the metal ladder to check on the condition of the mattress.

"A buffet is served every four hours on the hour, 'round the clock," Randy said as he laid his duffel bag on one of the lower bunks.

"You'll get fat if you take this job." John chimed in. "Nothing much to do during downtime except eat and sleep."

The food turned out to be good, and Thanksgiving lunch—turkey, dressing and all the trimmings—far

Flexibility | 51

exceeded my expectations. Sleeping was a whole different story, however. Because you're literally strapped onto the frame of that drill rig in the little plastic bunkhouse, when the drill bit hits a hard formation of rock, you're almost tossed out of the bed. It wasn't until the fifth night, our last night on the rig, that I finally got the hang of hanging on while sleeping.

After an unforgettable week spent learning the ins and outs of downhole geophysical sampling and testing, I was back on the chopper with John and Randy early Saturday morning, and by Sunday afternoon I was back in Raleigh.

Shortly after that trip to Louisiana, Schlumberger offered me a position as a geophysicist in its Houma, Louisiana, office. But at the time, the flexibility needed to work thirty-day shifts on an oil rig somewhere out in the Gulf just wasn't in my youthful makeup. I was flexible but not *that* flexible. I was a country boy from the mountains and just couldn't envision a life of nights spent sleeping in a horizontal Port-a-John strapped to some oil platform a hundred miles offshore. So I went back to Ellenboro and started a geological consulting company of my own.

How important is flexibility to a performance-based professional? I believe it's extremely important. In my case, I was flexible enough to change majors and follow my heart, and I was flexible enough to take a helicopter 145 miles offshore to spend a week on an oil rig on the spur of the moment, and it all served a purpose. I found out what I wanted and what I didn't want at that particular point in my career, and that clarity allowed me to pursue my career path in an efficient manner. Flexibility is also what ultimately led me to a position as head coach of a college fast-pitch softball team and my current position in the financial-services industry. And flexibility is what has gotten me through it all.

To give you an idea of what I'm talking about, consider a typical day in my life as a financial-services professional. I arrive at the office at 8 a.m., thirty minutes before we open, to get my proposals together for my ten o'clock appointment, make a few calls to schedule more appointments for next week and tidy up my office a bit. After that first appointment, during which I'll write up a big life-insurance case I've been working on for a couple of weeks, I'll schedule the paramedical exams, make copies of the apps and head to lunch around noon. At one, I'll be back in the office to prepare my files for two afternoon appointments for comprehensive insurance reviews, both of which I'm confident will produce additional business and possibly some referrals. A perfect game plan, right?

But then the doors open at eight-thirty and in walks a client, straight past the receptionist and into my office. It's Mr. Johnson. A talker and a retiree, he stops by regularly just to spend a few hours chatting. *Why today?* I extend my hand and welcome him.

He's carrying a stack of wrinkled papers—quotes and printouts and sales ads for boats and campers and motorcycles. "I don't know which one of these I'm going to buy," he says. "I want you to quote the insurance on each one and I'm going to base my decision on that."

I sit there stunned. *I can't believe this. I still have to prepare for the life case coming in at ten.* A queasiness rises from the depths of my stomach to the back of my throat. A boat, a motorcycle and a camper—three of the hardest things to run quotes on. *How am I going to handle this one?*

Then he says he wants to add comp and collision to his 2001 Ford Taurus and wants to get a price on that today, too. "And while you're at it, I need a binder for this old mobile home I just bought yesterday afternoon," he adds with an evil smile. "It doesn't have any coverage on it now."

That's half a day's worth of work, and my life appointment is in a little over an hour. *How am I going to handle this?*

"Mr. Johnson, I really appreciate you coming by to see me today. It's always a pleasure. Please have a seat and let's see what you've got there." In my profession and in my personal life, I try to treat everyone with fairness, dignity and respect, and no matter how inconvenient this meeting with my client may be, he's entitled to the same-quality service that every client deserves. "Mr. Johnson, if it's OK with you, here's what I would like to do. I have an appointment coming in at ten o'clock, and if you could leave me this information, I'll work on the quotes this afternoon and give you a call back before five. I want to make sure I've gotten you the absolute best price for each of these quotes."

Mr. Johnson smiles. He's very appreciative that I want to take care of his needs and hands me the stack of wrinkled papers.

"Now, Mr. Johnson, let's get some information on the mobile home that you purchased and talk about the pros and cons of adding that comp and collision to your Taurus. And when we finish up here, I want to talk to you about your life insurance needs. I've been meaning to contact you about your life insurance anyway." These policy changes will only take fifteen minutes or so, and I do want to talk with him about his life insurance needs anyway, so I seize the opportunity!

Sure, I could have stopped Mr. Johnson at the door, told him I was too busy to meet with him and ushered him back to his car, but how would he have felt about that meeting? Would he have recommended my services to his friends, or would he have told everyone in the county how rude I was to him? I suspect the latter. But because I've taken the time to take care of Mr. Johnson's needs, make him feel important and give him the service that every client deserves, he'll recommend me to his friends and family and maybe even to people he barely knows. Wouldn't you rather have an advocate for your services than an unhappy client who's bad-mouthing you all over town?

All it took was a little flexibility in my schedule to provide quality service to a client and gain an advocate for my business. What was fifteen minutes out of my day to provide a face-to-face service that will linger in my client's memory as a positive encounter? And I still had plenty of time to get my proposals ready for that big life insurance appointment at ten.

Face-to-face meetings with our clients should be treated as an opportunity. They spare us the time and effort of making all those calls to schedule appointments, so seize the opportunity. These surprises happen, as I'm sure you've noticed in your own career, and you can let it get to you and stress you out, or you can be flexible and roll with the punches.

Flexibility is critical to the performance-based professional. It's critical to your well-being and even your sanity. I learned early in life that things are rarely as you plan them to be, because God's plan for your life isn't quite the same as your own plan, and that goes for your day-to-day schedule, too. Maybe God put Mr. Johnson there in front of you today for a reason. Now it's up to you to make the best of that encounter.

Make a point to be more flexible in both your career and your personal life. You'll be a lot happier, and your family will, too.

5 DISCIPLINE

> "Do you not know that in a race, all runners run, but only one gets the prize? Run in such a way as to get the prize."
>
> —1 Corinthians 9:24

I'VE ALWAYS PLAYED SPORTS. As a kid growing up, I played Little League baseball and peewee football. In middle school, I played baseball and basketball, and in high school I played baseball and football and ran on the track team. As an adult, I played softball well into my thirties, until I got too old and those bumps and bruises didn't heal as fast as they once did. But after I hung up my cleats, I volunteered with the local Little League softball program as a coach and was soon asked to coach a local high school team. Ultimately, I was recruited to be an assistant coach at the collegiate level.

When I sold my independent insurance agency to a large conglomerate in 2007 and found myself longing for another challenge, I decided to pursue my love of sports and apply for a coaching position in fast-pitch softball. I polished my resume, sent it to a handful of large colleges and hoped someone would respond with an offer. At the time, I was about halfway through an online master's degree program in business management with a concentration in sports management, and a coaching career at the collegiate level would be the perfect marriage of my business skills and my passion for sports.

In the summer, I got a call from Coach Beverly Smith from the University of North Carolina at Chapel Hill. The school was looking for an assistant coach for the Lady Tar Heel softball program, and she wanted me to come in for an interview with her and legendary Coach Donna Papa. This was great! I could work as a graduate assistant coach with the softball program and possibly complete an internship with the athletics department for my master's degree at the same time.

As it turned out, I was offered both the position as an assistant coach and an internship with the athletic department, and the experience was a life-changing one. The coaching and life strategies I learned from Coaches Papa, Smith, and Janelle Brenneman were inspiring and a major boost for me in many ways. They gave me insight into what it takes to be a successful collegiate coach, a top-level recruiter and a much better person.

In early 2008, just after the Tar Heels had finished their fall season, I got a call from the athletic director at Meredith College, in Raleigh, North Carolina. She'd heard I was interested in a head coaching position in collegiate softball and asked me to send her a resume. Over the next month, I interviewed with the athletic director, the associate athletic director, the dean of the physical education department and the college president. I was offered the job in late January, and on February 23, 2008, I was standing in the dugout for my first NCAA softball game as a head coach. We won that game against Sweet Briar College on a walk-off two-run homer in the bottom of the seventh—a moment I'll never forget. I still have the official game ball sitting on my desk today.

Over my three seasons at Meredith College, our staff transformed the softball program from a struggling, wayward, undisciplined and unrespected program to one of the most respected, most disciplined and most feared teams in our conference and in our region. And it was no easy feat. The team had been a cellar dweller for the better part of a decade and had no confidence whatsoever. The players practiced when they wanted to and showed up to play when they wanted to, and if they didn't feel like it, that was OK. It wasn't that they didn't want to win or that they were losing on purpose. They simply had no discipline and no faith that they could win.

This happens a lot in every area of life. Think about the people you know who are down on their luck. Losing becomes a habit—an almost impossible one to break. Losing is easy, winning is hard. Many people would rather take it easy and lose than put in the hard work and win. And to break the habit of losing, the first thing that has to be instilled in them is discipline.

"Discipline is discipline is discipline is discipline!!!" I'd preach to my players on a daily basis, and I'm sure those words are still ringing in their ears today.

"There's no difference in discipline," I'd continue. "You use the same discipline to make sure your alarm clock is set in the morning, to make sure you get to class on time, to make sure your homework is turned in, to make sure you have all your gear when you get to practice, to make sure you're on the bus when we pull out to go to the game, to make sure you eat right and are in bed at a decent hour. And you use that same discipline to lay off that ball-four pitch when it's way outside. You use that same discipline to know which base to throw the ball to every single time you field a play—not sometimes but every time. You use that same discipline to stay on first base to see a line drive through the infield so you don't get picked off for a double play if the outfielder makes a play on the ball in the air."

It's all the same discipline. If you have discipline in sports, you're well on your way to winning games, and if you have discipline in your life, you're well on your

Discipline | 61

way to success. In sports and in life, discipline can't be an occasional thing if you want to succeed. It has to be an all-the-time thing. If you don't have the discipline to lay off that ball-four pitch when it's way outside, you probably won't have the discipline necessary to succeed in your career either. It's all about discipline.

We transformed that Meredith College softball program into a winning team filled with pride, self-confidence and self-discipline. We had our first winning record in 2009 and won our first conference tournament game in 2010. Three of my recruits went on to break many of the USA South Athletic Conference records in hitting and pitching and were selected for the USA South's fiftieth-anniversary all-conference team for their accomplishments. We were living proof that with a lot of hard work and self-discipline, the habit of losing can be broken.

Most of us at least have the self-discipline to get up and go to work every morning. At the office, we pull out our keys, unlock the door, walk in and sit at our desk. But then comes the fateful decision: "Now what am I going to do?" That's where we *really* need discipline. It's the first fork in the road that we as salesmen or managers or production-oriented professionals confront whenever we walk into the office. We stand at the fork in that long dusty road trying to decide whether to take the path of least resistance. You know, the path most traveled, where we could spend a large part of our day gossiping with office mates, surfing the web and otherwise trying to get out of work.

"Hey, if we take that path, there are all kinds of fun things we can do," the little devil on our right shoulder says. "We can read the newspaper we picked up on the way into the office. We can check the new posts on our Facebook page. We can peruse the latest videos on YouTube. Heck, we can even shop online at our favorite stores." So many things to do, so little time. Or we can take the path much less traveled. You know, the path that actually requires some effort from us, the path that requires us to get some things done and allows us to be productive in both our personal and professional lives.

"C'mon, we only have two weeks left in this month's production contest," the little angel on our left shoulder says. "The deadline for our big project is only two weeks away. We have to make some calls to set up some sales appointments this morning."

Does this scenario ring true for you? Do you or some of your co-workers wage a daily battle with the ol' conscience? How do those battles turn out? Like 1 Corinthians says, there are a lot of runners running in your race—both inside and outside your company—and winning these battles can separate you from the pack.

To achieve that, there's a particular weapon you'll need to have in your arsenal: discipline. Luckily, it's a character trait that can be learned and perfected. We just have to know what it looks like so we can emulate it and get better at it. And it all starts with understanding that the decisions we make at the office have a direct effect on the standard of living we provide for our families. We always hear that you need to separate your work life from your family life, that you can't take your work home with you. Well, if you're in a performance-based career, there's no separating family from work. If you aren't working or aren't spending your time at work in a productive manner, your family is absolutely going to suffer the consequences of your actions.

Now, don't get me wrong. I firmly believe that we all need to have a balanced life and that quality time with your spouse and your family is vitally important to your sanity and overall health. Work and family *should* be separate in the sense that you give your family 100 percent of your focus when you're with them. But they *can't* be separate in the sense that the level of self-discipline you bring to your work directly affects your family's standard of living and, in turn, the quality of your quality time together.

Let me give you an example. I unlock the office door, set my briefcase down next to my desk, turn on my computer and pull out the newspaper and start reading through the headlines. Thirty minutes later—I'd gotten so engrossed in the daily gazette that I forgot all about signing into my corporate account—I enter my password into my log-in screen, and while it's booting up my office programs, I move on to the sports page. I peruse the major league box scores and check out the headlines about the opening-day lineups. *Wonder if Tiger's back will let him compete in the Masters ... Nice, an editorial about next week's NFL draft.* Another twenty minutes later, I move my mouse to click on our corporate software—you know, where all the files of work waiting to be done are located. But first I need to check the classifieds. I'm looking for a new fishing boat for spring.

Finally, an hour after sitting at my desk and pushing the power button on my computer, I lay the newspaper down and check my company e-mail.

Sound familiar?

If this is your daily routine—and we haven't even accounted for getting a cup of coffee, stopping by to say hello to your office mates or eating the bacon, egg and cheese biscuit and hash browns you picked up on your way in—think about how much potentially productive time you waste in a year.

At a rate of one wasted hour a day five days a week, if you work fifty weeks a year, that's 250 wasted hours a year—the equivalent of 6¼ workweeks. Staggering, huh? *More than six weeks a year.* An eighth of your entire production year gone. In terms of your family's standard of living, that's at least a couple of vacations at choice destinations.

> ### Simple Time Study I:
>
> (1) hour per day × (5) working days per week = (5) hours per week
>
> (5) hours per week × (50) weeks per year = (250) wasted hours per year
>
> (250) hours divided by a normal (40) hour week = 6.25 wasted weeks a year!!!

If you're planning to win a race, is this a constructive use of your valuable time? Are your competitors wasting this much time? In a production-based career, can you really afford to lose 6¼ weeks of production?

Time management is a concept we're all familiar with. You may even represent a company that completes some type of time study on you or your departments on an annual basis. But sometimes familiar concepts are *so* familiar that we become numb to them. We forget how important they are to our success as performance-based professionals. We forget how critical time management is. In both life and performance-based careers like sales, what's the one thing you absolutely can't get back when it's gone? Time. You can never get back those moments you waste doing something unproductive. And over the course of a career, those moments really add up.

Let's look again at the scenario where one potentially productive hour is wasted every day. At a rate of 250 wasted hours a year, in a thirty-year career that adds up to 7,500 hours. That's the equivalent of 3¾ years, assuming a standard work year of 2,000 hours. And assuming a potential performance-based salary of $100,000 a year, that works out to $375,000 that's left behind, which doesn't even take into account the time value of money.

> **Simple Time Study II:**
>
> (250) hours per year × (30) year career = (7500) hours
>
> (7500) hours divided by (2000) hours = 3.75 wasted years in a 30-year career (using 2,000 hours per year as a standard work year)
>
> (3.75 years) × $100,000 per year = $375,000 wasted over a 30-year career

How much do you have in your retirement account? That $375,000 would look pretty sweet in there right now, I bet.

At this point, maybe you're admitting to yourself that you do spend a little time at work in the unproductive mode. What to do about it?

Start by being conscious of every moment of your workday. Conduct a time study of every single moment. On a legal-size notepad, devote a page to each day of the week and record your days in fifteen-minute increments. The time should appear in the left margin, and how you spend that time should be explained in detail in the body portion of the page. It should look something like this:

8:00 a.m. Turned on the computer and went to the break room to pour myself a cup of coffee.
8:15 a.m. Looked over my contact list for potential clients to call today. Made the first call to John Smith to schedule an appointment for Thursday.
8:30 a.m. Fred, my suite mate, stopped by my office to talk about last night's NCAA basketball tournament games and the office pool.
8:45 a.m. Fred still sitting in my office when my phone rings. I take the call and speak with Mrs. Johnson about her annuity, which will mature next month.
9:00 a.m. Made a call to the second name on my contact list …

I'd recommend that you conduct your time study for at least a week, but doing it for a month will give you a more comprehensive sampling from which to draw conclusions. When you're done, use a green (the color of money) highlighter marker to highlight each time period that you consider productive time, time when your actions were devoted to earning money. Then use a red highlighter (representing the things that make you stop earning money) to highlight all the time segments that you consider to be wasted time. Now hold up your pages and you'll see a great visual representation of how productive or unproductive your time at work is. Do you have more green or more red? Tally up the unproductive minutes in a week and use that figure to determine the amount of money you're likely to lose in a month, in a year and over your career based on your current or projected income levels. Multiply the weekly wasted hours by fifty to determine the loss for the year, and multiply that figure by the expected length of your career.

Hard to believe, isn't it? All that income you could have had …

Sometimes the truth is hard to stomach. For some of you, it will be difficult to be honest in your assessment of your productivity and take a hard look at your time management. But being totally honest with yourself is critical to your success in both the long term and the short term. In fact, getting it all down on paper and acknowledging how your time management is directly affecting not only your success but your family's standard of living is 90 percent of the battle. After all, if you don't recognize the problem, how can you correct it?

Over the years, many professionals have told me that much of their day is spent in a whirlpool of busywork. You know, the blender that whips up a mix of one part office drama, one part client-perceived emergency, one part improper time management and one part inability to say "no." It's a foamy concoction called "It's five o'clock and I didn't get a thing done all day," and the truth is, we've all drunk it. But the good thing is that the way you spend your day is your choice. You make the choice when you turn on your computer in the morning and stand in front of the first crossroads of the day, with productivity down one path and wasted time down the other.

And make no mistake—the "time sucks" that can rob you of precious time you'll never get back are lurking everywhere, and it's critical that you recognize who and what they are. Is it Fred, who wants to bend your ear about last night's basketball game? Is it the unread newspaper trying to get your attention on the corner of your desk? Is it the Internet, with its endless shopping possibilities? Whatever they are, your success depends on finding ways to overcome their threats to your productivity.

In other words, you need to reorganize your daily routine in a way that allows you to get as much done as possible. And based on the information that your time study revealed, that should be easily accomplished.

One way to do it is by making a daily schedule for yourself and following it strictly for at least six months. The details of this written "daily time map" should include, at minimum, structured plans for the way you spend your time on the job each day. For example, for financial planners, blocks of time should be set aside for activities such as marketing, scheduling appointments, following up on underwriting issues and completing paperwork that's an essential part of their business.

As you reorganize—or revitalize—your routine, try to schedule the activities you dread the most for early in the day. If returning messages is the daily task you like the least, knock it out in the first block. Imagine the productive mind-set you'll bring to the rest of the day if you get those calls out of the way first!

Mornings aren't always the answer, though. Friday afternoons are great for setting up appointments for the next week, for example. If that's one of your least favorite tasks, you might be surprised at how satisfying it can be to tackle it right after lunch on Friday. You can start your weekend knowing that you put the afternoon to good use and that you have a full calendar of appointments scheduled for the next week. It's also *easier* to set up appointments on Friday afternoons because clients tend to be in better moods then and more eager to commit to appointments than they are on Monday mornings. Whatever tricks you use, remember that the goal is to make your workweek as enjoyable and stress-free as possible so that it can also be as productive as possible.

So, to review, first we have to conduct a time study to identify the "time sucks" that sneak into our lives on a daily basis. Then, once we've developed an acute awareness of how we spend every moment of our days, we need to develop a very structured weekly schedule in which blocks of time are allocated to particular areas of our work that require attention every day. And while we're at it, let's schedule those time blocks in the manner that gives us the most productive mind-set possible. Simple, right?

Well, if you have your doubts, rest assured that all it takes is discipline. And once you get into the habit and start enjoying its rewards, you just may find that there's no turning back.

6 RESILIENCE

> "I have told you these things, so that in me you may have peace. In this world you will have trouble. But take heart! I have overcome the world."
>
> —John 16:33

After the plane came to a stop on the taxiway, my instructor unlatched his seat belt, opened his door and stepped onto the hot North Carolina blacktop.

"Good luck! Bring her back in one piece," Jeff said as he latched the door and turned to walk back up to the terminal building.

It was the moment I'd worked so diligently for, and it was also the moment I'd dreaded for so long. Almost in a mild state of shock, I sat there in the heat of the little cockpit for a moment, the persistent hum of the propellers seeming to say, "C'mon, man, what are you waiting on?"

I reflected on the last eight weeks of pilot training. Hours of practice had been required to get me to this moment in my career as a private pilot—my first solo flight. I clearly recalled the first day I'd crawled into the tiny cockpit for my first takeoff with my instructor. I remember the adrenaline rush I experienced when the wheels separated from the asphalt and the fear I felt when we pointed the plane back toward the Shelby, North Carolina, airport and Jeff jokingly said, "OK, she's yours. Land her."

I remembered practicing crosswind takeoffs and landings. "9388Xray, turning final to runway 23 Shelby," I announced as we made the left turn toward our final approach during our tenth crosswind landing of the session—my tenth white-knuckle attempt to sit a light little two-seater down with the wind trying to blow us off the other side of the runway. "The only way you're gonna get good at it is to do it over and over," Jeff said as we circled the airport at eight hundred feet for what seemed like hours.

Just like with helicopters, a majority of airplane accidents occur during takeoffs and landings, and those are some of the hardest things to learn about flying. By the time you get to the crosswind practice, with a wind that's blowing across the runway at an angle other than straight down the pipe, you've probably completed seventy-five to a hundred normal takeoffs and landings with your instructor. On that particular day, we had a twenty- to twenty-five-knot crosswind with gusts of thirty-five to forty knots—right at the limit of what the little Cessna 152 could handle.

"Crab it in, Robert. Drop your left wing slightly. You're doing good." Jeff always had such confidence in his voice, a confidence that usually left *me* feeling confident, but not this time. "A little more left rudder. Line it up to the center. You're at two hundred feet, doing good!"

And then, out of nowhere, a gust of at least forty-five knots blindsided my high wing and flipped the Cessna like a pinwheel at the beach. For a split-second, I was looking at the end of the runway upside down. The adrenaline of fear swept through my veins.

But before my fight-or-flight instinct could even kick in, we were back upright, throttle hammer down. Jeff was in full control of the airplane, using the radio to announce a go-around to the other air traffic in the area. We gained altitude again and put the runway behind us in preparation for another try.

"No barrel rolls on final approach," Jeff said in his calm, confident, commanding voice. He smiled.

As I made the turn to the downwind leg of the approach, I felt like crying or maybe throwing up.

"If you don't mind, try to keep it upright this time," Jeff said, smirking now.

As it turned out, touchdown went smoothly on this final attempt of the day, and the terminal building was a welcome sight as we taxied up the slight grade to our parking spot.

But that was a different day. Today's sky was crisp and blue, like on many early-fall days in western North Carolina, and the sun warmed the cockpit as I sat there on the taxiway gathering my thoughts before rolling off. Like a roulette wheel spinning through each number, all my takeoffs and landings turned through my mind.

"You'd be good on an aircraft carrier," Jeff would say when I'd come in a little fast, or "hot." "The runway is divided into thirds, my friend. Your third is the first third. My third is the second third. The last third is God's third ... You don't want to land on God's third."

When you come in too hot, the ground effect—a cushion of air between the ground and the wings—won't allow the wheels to touch down, and while you're bleeding off some of that speed, you're swiftly being carried toward God's third. And once you're on God's third, there's precious little room left to come to a stop.

That was just one of the mistakes I made in the hundreds of times—literally hundreds—that I'd taken this little plane off and landed it in preparation for this moment. Time and time and time again, I'd failed in some little aspect of my landings and Jeff wasn't comfortable with letting me go up by myself. But my resilience was finally paying its dividends. Today I'd slicked it in perfectly for eight or ten landings in a row, and after the last one Jeff let himself out and gave me his blessing. The time for my first solo flight had finally arrived. And after sitting on the runway for what seemed like an hour but was probably only five minutes, I cleared my mind of all the memories of past takeoffs and landings and focused my thoughts on the task at hand. I eased the throttle knob forward and pointed the Cessna toward the downwind end of the runway. "9388 Xray departing 23 Shelby," I announced over the radio with a confidence I'd never felt before in that cockpit. My left foot pushed the rudder pedal to the floor, and the little plane spun a 180 from the taxiway onto the end of the runway, pointing into the oncoming breeze.

The huge white "23" painted on the runway to indicate 230 degrees on the compass had been there to witness every one of my takeoffs and landings. Only Jeff and I and the big "23" on the runway knew how much work had gone into this day. Now that "23" seemed to smile at me as if to say, "You can do this! I know you can."

In one motion, I pushed the throttle knob all the way to the dashboard. The yoke began to feel lighter as the Cessna picked up speed down the five thousand-foot runway. In my head, as clear as if he were beside me, I could hear Jeff giving me instructions. "A little left rudder. Straight down the runway. Pull back ... easy. Ten degrees." And just like that, the wheels were off the ground and I was flying—all alone!

First solo flights are brief, though, and it was already time to head back down. At eight hundred feet in altitude, I eased off the throttle to seventy knots, turned the yoke to the left, gave it a little left rudder and lined myself up on the downwind approach to the landing. Looking down to my left, I could see the little Shelby airport, the "23" marker on the runway looking like a beacon. I could also see Jeff and the airport's manager of fixed-base operations looking up to watch me.

"Bring her home in one piece," I could hear Jeff say in my head. "Ten degrees of flaps, sixty knots, get ready for crosswind."

"9388Xray ... Final approach to 23 Shelby," I said as I made my left turn to final approach. "Fifty knots, another ten degrees of flaps ... and ... no barrel rolls on final!" I smiled to myself and lined her up on that big "23" at the end of the runway.

I have to land on my end of the runway. Can't make it to God's end.

As the Cessna floated over "23" and the first set of stripes, I lined the nose up with the other end, felt the ground effects and slicked those three little wheels right onto the sun-soaked blacktop. Finally, my heart left its temporary location in my throat and returned to its normal position.

Whew.

My arms were so weak I could hardly engage the throttle to taxi up to the terminal building, where Jeff was waiting for me.

"Congratulations," he said. "You did a great job. And you brought her back in one piece." He shook my hand and hugged me at the same time.

"And I didn't do a barrel roll on my final approach," I said with a big smile. I was so excited and relieved at the same time that I couldn't decide whether to laugh or kiss the ground.

I handed Jeff my pilot's logbook, and he promptly turned me around, took out a pair of scissors and cut the back out of the T-shirt I was wearing. It's pilot protocol to have your shirttail cut off when you complete your first solo. I was more than happy to drive back home that day wearing only half a shirt. It certainly beat the alternative.

Learning to fly was something I'd always wanted to do. It was so important to me, that I was willing to go through all the necessary trials and tribulations to make it a reality. Going to that airport week in and week out and endlessly practicing takeoffs and landings took a tremendous amount of resilience. Until the day I was ready to solo, it was all about making mistakes and bouncing back from them. Making mistakes over and over and bouncing back over and over. And finally it all paid off. My first solo flight was in the books.

Now imagine if we could take that level of resilience to work with us every day. Being able to withstand setbacks and rejection is a vital part of my job description as a professional in the financial-services industry. You can't let setbacks get you down.

An agency manager once told me something that changed the way I looked at my job and my life. "Robert," he said, "you are paid in direct proportion to the amount of rejection that you can withstand every day," Truer words were never spoken. Think about it. Sales- and performance-based businesses are driven by numbers, specifically the numbers of potential clients contacted every day. The more contacts you make every day—sales calls, home visits, appointments—the more rejections you're going to get every day *and* the more sales you'll close every day. They go hand in hand. If you doubled or tripled the number of rejections you get every day, just imagine how many more sales you'd close by the end of the month!

As a performance-based professional, you have to get outside your comfort zone. You have to do some barrel rolls on final approach and make some aircraft-carrier landings to make you a better pilot. And you have to be resilient. Let the setbacks be lessons to you, and turn those lessons into success. You can't get better without practice. The more takeoffs and landings you execute, the smoother those landings will become.

After I moved into management in the life insurance industry, I began to train and mentor young agents who were new to the business. I always stressed to them that our industry is a "numbers game" and that the number of written applications and closed sales would be directly dependent on the number of appointments they had on a daily basis. Often, a new agent would say, "Well, I went through my list of life insurance prospects and didn't set any appointments." My response? "Well, then you need a bigger list!"

When your business relies on numbers, you truly are paid in direct proportion to the amount of rejection you can withstand. To be successful, you have to see and meet with a lot of people, and being rejected is just part of the equation—one of the barrel rolls you have to get through to be successful. Resilience is the key for the performance-based professional. Shake off the barrel rolls, take a deep breath and get right back to it.

Remember, it's a numbers game. The more rejections you get, the more success you'll have. And the more resilient you are, the more rejections you can withstand!

7 CONFIDENCE

> "For the Lord will be your confidence and will keep your foot from being snared."
> —Proverbs 3:26

> "Such confidence as this is ours through Christ before God. Not that we are competent in ourselves to claim anything for ourselves, but our competence comes from God."
> —2 Corinthians 3:4-5

It was a crisp mid-February morning in northern Florida. Our drive down from North Carolina the day before had been uneventful, the monotony broken up only by occasional stops at rest areas and truck stops for Big Gulps and coffee. Because we were pulling a trailer, it took about eight hours rather than seven, and we rolled into the hotel around six-thirty. Once we'd all checked in, we grabbed a quick burger and turned in for the night. It was hard to fall asleep, though, kind of like on Christmas Eve when I used to wait for Santa's arrival.

I'd set the alarm for 5 a.m., but the excitement woke me long before that. I peeped around the curtains and into the parking lot—nothing but darkness and a few lone streetlights. By five-thirty, I was standing in the chilly morning air waiting for the sun to rise and wishing my crew would hurry up and get down here. We'd been preparing for this day since November, and now that it was finally here, I could hardly contain myself. The big safety gate to the garage was scheduled to open at seven, and I wanted to be first in line to get in.

At seven on the dot, the track official swung open the gate and motioned for our line of big-rig car haulers to make its way to the infield garage. As we crossed the threshold onto that hallowed ground, my mind raced with thoughts of all the great NASCAR finishes that had happened right here during my childhood. The Petty-Pearson finish, when David Pearson won the race in a wrecked race car and Richard Petty's crew pushed his car across the finish line. The late-'90s Earnhardt-Waltrip battles in the Daytona 500. And how about the Allison Brothers and Cale Yarborough duking it out in the grass after a late-race crash took them all out of contention?

At over two hundred miles per hour, all my racing heroes had crossed the finish line that lay just a quarter mile from where I was standing. I'd watched these guys race since my early childhood in western North Carolina, when I would root for Petty just to antagonize my father, whose favorite driver was Pearson.

A big-time racing fan, my father often told me of his friendships with Fireball Roberts and Ned Jarrett and took me to the speedways at Charlotte, Daytona and Darlington and the short track at North Wilkesboro. Mesmerized by the roar and blur of those old-school racers passing by at warp speed as we sat in the infield on the hood of his old Plymouth, I dreamed of being a race-car driver someday—a dream my mom didn't support at all. But such were the ambitions of boys who grew up in the heart of NASCAR country, where watching the Saturday-night short-track races was as routine as going to church on Sunday morning.

After my father passed away, I went on to race myself, and here I finally was at Daytona International Speedway on a winter's day in 1997, filled with awe and feeling engulfed by history, including my own. It had been a long road to this day, after all.

For over six years, I'd put in my time at Hickory and Tri-County speedways, and for most of that period my evenings were spent turning wrenches, changing springs and painting fenders to get ready for the weekly short-track event. A year before, though, I made the decision to move up from the late-model series to the Goody's Dash, a full-fledged NASCAR touring series that followed the Bush Grand National and Winston Cup series to tracks across the Southeast. NASCAR rules don't allow a new driver to show up at Daytona and just roll out to practice without a certain level of experience—for safety reasons, both he and NASCAR have to be confident of his abilities—and after I'd driven in five short-track races in the Dash series the prior year, NASCAR gave me the OK to come down to try to qualify.

To signal to the other drivers that I was a rookie, my crew chief and I had put the famous yellow duct tape on the rear bumper of my bright blue and orange Pontiac. Daytona was known to be hard on rookies—the track seemed to have the ability to sense fear, the kind of fear that predators sense in their prey—and the yellow stripe just heightened the intimidation I was feeling. The tri-oval track seemed to stretch endlessly. In the distance, the front stretch narrowed into an asphalt ribbon that ultimately disappeared into turn one, where the banking was as tall as a three-story building. And turn two looked like it was in another county.

"How in the world can you run three cars side by side going into that turn?" I said to Rodney, my crew chief, as we pulled down the pit road toward the garage area.

"You'll figure it out," he said.

It took an hour or so to unload the car, the pit cart and our equipment from the big hauler, and then we moved it all into the assigned Goody's Dash garage space. While the crew readied the car for inspection,

I attended a meeting for rookie drivers and took a lap around the track in the pace car with other rookies. NASCAR officials don't want your first time around the track to be at 180 miles per hour, so they gave us an 80-mph tour in the pace car. Afterward, we returned to the garage area, where my crew had finished up the trip through NASCAR inspection, put on a set of sticker tires and loaded the Pontiac with fuel. I crawled through the window and settled into the narrow confines of the padded racing seat.

"Crank it up," Rodney said in an almost-giddy tone. "Let's go see what we got!"

I made one last tug on my seat belts and snugged up the chin strap of my helmet, checked the window net and eased off the clutch to back out of the garage area.

Finally, the moment was here—my first laps on the Daytona speedway. And I couldn't have been more confident in my car. Rodney and the crew had been preparing it since mid-October. The aerodynamic body had been hung on the chassis by one of the best in the business. The rear end had been set up just for this track. Every piece of the car was brand-new: the transmission, the shocks, the engine, the springs, the fuel cell, everything. And to make sure there were no hairline fractures that could cause a calamity at high speed, we'd magna-fluxed every suspension part, spindle, hub, wheel, A-frame, tie rod and any other part that could crack or fracture.

"Make a couple laps around the inside and let's get the engine warmed up," Rodney instructed over the radio as I turned out of the garage area and onto the long pit road. "Make sure nothing is going to fall off before you get up to speed."

"Thanks, Rodney. I sure hope nothing's going to fall off," I said, knowing he was just kidding to loosen me up. He'd been here as a crew chief for other teams—his father, Roger, who was also on my crew, had even raced at Daytona in this same series—so they knew what I was feeling.

After making a couple of laps on the bottom of the high banks, we got the green flag signaling that practice was officially underway. Other drivers who'd been part of the warm-up line around the bottom, accelerated and streaked by me down the front stretch and off into the asphalt unknown that was the turn one banking.

"You ready?" Rodney said. "Let's see what we got."

Steadily, I pressed the accelerator toward the metal floorboard, hearing the engine sing as the RPM needle rose on the tach gauge directly in front of me. I shifted into fourth gear as I came through the tri-oval.

I'm racing at Daytona!

As I entered the steep banking of turn one where the drivers ahead of me had disappeared, I relaxed the pressure on the throttle because that's what you normally do when you enter a banked turn. But I quickly realized I should be back on the gas. The turn was big enough and the banking steep enough that I didn't need to slow down, and all I was doing was losing time. So I floored it and my blue rocket ship blasted out of turn two and down the mile-long superstretch.

And then I saw turn three. It looked even more narrow and more daunting than turn one.

But I was determined. *I'm holding it down all the way through this time!*

As it turned out, my brain and my right foot were in direct conflict as to how long to keep the accelerator pressed. My brain was saying, "Back off," but my foot was proving to be pretty heavy.

I knew that at Daytona, when you're out there by yourself and not in a draft with another car, you can hold down the throttle all the way through the turns, but that goes against everything I'd learned on the short tracks of western North Carolina. At the Hickory Speedway, it takes only fifteen seconds to complete a lap. You're completely off the throttle going into the turn and don't pick it back up until you're pointed in the other direction coming out of the turn. In my experience, it just wasn't normal to hold the throttle to the floorboard around the entire length of a speedway. But I was going to do it this time anyway!

And I did. As a result, I qualified for the Discount Auto Parts 250 in my first attempt at Daytona, and on February 15, 1997, I finished the race in a respectable fifteenth place in a field of forty-three drivers who started the race. If you look up the word *confidence* in a dictionary, the definition will be something to the effect of "the feeling that a race-car driver has toward his car, his seat belts, his helmet, his tires and his crew that allows him to hold the accelerator to the floor all the way through a turn at Daytona International Speedway."

It takes an awful lot of confidence to make a lap around that 2½-mile track without lifting the accelerator pedal. And it takes even more confidence to run that same speed among forty-three other cars, nose to tail, side by side, inches or less from one another as you enter blind banked turns so steep you can't even walk up them.

As unlikely as it sounds, it takes the same confidence to unlock the door to your office and begin your workday. Or at least it takes the same confidence to begin your workday the *right* way. Nothing breeds success more than confidence, and nothing can lead to your failure quicker than a lack of it. Think about it. If I hadn't had confidence in my car, my tires, my safety equipment and my crew, I could never have talked myself into flat-footing the accelerator around that speedway. And if I hadn't flat-footed it, I wouldn't have qualified for the race, because my speed would have been too slow, and I wouldn't have finished in the top fifteen as a rookie competitor. Without confidence, my trip to Daytona would have been a failure.

Do you believe your co-workers and your employees can sense the level of confidence you have in them? Do you believe your clients can sense the level of confidence you have in the product you're selling? They absolutely can. As a life insurance agent, it's imperative that I have resounding confidence in myself, in my company and in the products I recommend for my clients. Insurance agents sell a contract, an intangible product. You can't feel it. You can't see it. You can't smell it. What we sell is a promise. We sell confidence in our companies and a promise that if our clients experience the loss of loved ones, we'll come through for them. We sell confidence that our companies and we as agents will be there to protect their standard of living at the worst time of their lives.

If you aren't confident in your product, how do you expect to sell it? If you don't believe in what you're selling, how do you expect to persuade someone else to buy it? If you aren't confident in your company, how can you convince potential clients that *they* should have confidence in it? Most important, if you aren't confident in *yourself*, how on earth do you expect a client to have confidence in you? It just can't happen. To be successful in business and in life, you have to have confidence in yourself.

Take control of the things in your life that are costing you your confidence. If you're worried that your tires will blow out going into turn one, change the tires. If you aren't sure your crew has tightened every bolt or made sure the lug nuts are on tight, spend some more time with them going over your expectations to build confidence in every member of your team. If they aren't getting the job done, maybe it's because we haven't put forth a true understanding of our expectations of them. Maybe their confidence level isn't as high as it should be because we haven't sufficiently trained them to meet those expectations. And in cases where crew members just aren't operating at a superspeedway performance level, you may need to change them out. As performance-based professionals, we are where the rubber meets the road. We have to have confidence in ourselves, in our company and in our products. Many people rely on our confidence and our ability to get the job done, no matter what the circumstances are. They expect us to be able to hold the accelerator down all the way through the corner. Without confidence in yourself and your team, you won't be able to do it. Think about the level of confidence you have in the service that you provide on a daily basis and consider this question: *Would you have confidence in you if you were your client?*

I challenge you to take a deep look inside yourself. Check your tires, your shocks, your engine, your safety belts and your helmet. Evaluate your crew chief and your crew. If what you find doesn't give you the necessary confidence to hold the throttle down all the way through the corner, maybe it's time to make a change, a change in yourself or your crew or maybe in the way you conduct your business.

Only you know what your level of confidence is, and only you can change it. If it isn't what you want it to be, let go of whatever is holding you back. To win your race, confidence is an absolute must. Crank it up and take those curves full-throttle!

8 PURPOSE

> "The Lord will fulfill his purpose for me, your love, O Lord, endures forever. Do not abandon the works of your hands."
>
> —PSALM 138:8

SHEEP ARE SOME interesting animals. They aren't the brightest beasts God created, but they're quite clever in their own right. I started raising sheep on a small farm in Rutherford County, North Carolina, in 1993 as a hobby for myself and my daughter. We began with ten or so ewes that we could show at the county and state fairs. I'd never raised sheep or any other grass-eating, multi-stomach farm animal, and their idiosyncrasies intrigued me. The thing that struck me first was their level of helplessness. Other than a shepherd or a guard animal, they have no means of protection from predators. When faced with danger, they might choose to run, but they're very slow animals compared with coyotes and mountain lions. Or they may pack tightly together in a group in an attempt to sacrifice one of the outside animals to save the rest of the flock. But more often than not, when faced with insurmountable odds, they just put their heads down, close their eyes partway and get ready to take their punishment.

So if you raise sheep in areas where there are predators, which could be anything from a coyote to a black bear to a bobcat to the neighbor's Labrador retriever, it's essential that you have some type of protection for them. Electric fencing is good, woven wire can be effective and even a guard donkey or llama will work in some areas. But my choice has always been guard dogs.

On my ranch here in Colorado, I have about seventy sheep of a meat breed known as Dorpers, and they have lots of predators—all the ones I mentioned above and then some. Without a well-conditioned guard dog like my Great Pyrenees, Bruno, my flock of Dorpers would be decimated in a week or so. Bruno is literally their salvation. He's the shepherd, the protector, the thinker and the provider for the flock. Without him, I couldn't have sheep.

When I started giving some thought to how I wanted to end this book, I knew I wanted to devote the last chapter to the subject of purpose. Without a purpose in your life, the seven other qualities I focus on in these pages are like soldiers without anything to fight for. Having a purpose is what ties everything together. After all, what is success—in your career or in your life—without a true purpose, without an internal calling to do what you were meant to do?

And that's where Bruno comes in. He stands at the top of the hill on my ranch, overlooking the flock grazing across the rolling grassy hills against the backdrop of the Rocky Mountains, absolutely knowing his purpose. Bruno knows that without his leadership, without his guidance, protection and oversight, those sheep would be gone in no time. Bruno has no doubt why he was put on this earth. His purpose is to protect those sheep, with his life if necessary.

And his purpose is what allows him to put his other strengths to use. Take his sense of discipline, for example. He follows the flock all day long every day of the year, never straying from their grazing paths. And he does it no matter how much he might prefer to be napping. He may be out there under a shade tree trying to catch some afternoon winks, with seventy-plus sheep gathered around him, when suddenly one sheep decides the grass looks greener a few hundred yards down the hill and under another tree. The whole flock will stand up, shake off and follow the independent thinker down the hill to the next tree, and though Bruno might want to sleep just a few more minutes before following them, he has too much discipline for that. He rouses himself from his slumber, follows the sheep to their chosen destination, and lies under the tree in the middle of them to resume his nap.

Bruno is also flexible and resilient. Wherever the sheep decide to take a break is fine with him. He'll find a comfortable spot nearby, usually at a slightly higher elevation and upwind of the flock so that he can see and smell a coyote if one should approach. And he doesn't let Colorado's extreme weather conditions take him out of the game. He's as resilient on an eastern-plains 100-degree summer day as he is on a twenty-below day with heavy blowing snow.

Confidence and tenacity? Absolutely! One evening around dusk, I heard a pack of coyotes howling and barking in the corner of the pasture, and as the ruckus grew closer, Bruno took off toward them, barking at the top of his lungs. I couldn't see what happened after he disappeared into a distant ravine, but I could hear plenty—snarling, growling, yelping. About five minutes later, Bruno pranced back toward the house, tail in the air and with a big smile on his face. Along the way, he marked every tree and fence post he passed to reinforce that this was his territory, just in case the coyotes hadn't picked up on that.

I looked him over for injuries, but there wasn't so much as a drop of blood. Somehow, without bringing harm to himself, he'd scared the coyotes off so effectively that we haven't heard from them since. Of course, it doesn't hurt that Bruno is the size of a small horse—his head reaches the top of my chest when he stands flat-footed—but it still requires a whole lot of confidence and tenacity to take on a pack of wild animals.

Bruno's no slouch when it comes to diligence, either. When he found himself in a quandary during our recent lambing season here on the ranch, it was his diligence that saw him—and the entire flock—through. The problem: When a ewe goes into labor, she'll separate herself from the flock, often at a great distance. She'll scratch out a little clearing under a tree on a high ridge at the top of the pasture and lie down and start pushing out the lamb. Well, Bruno knew he couldn't leave one sheep all alone in the pasture, unguarded. That's a surefire way to provoke a coyote attack on either the ewe, the new lamb or both. But Bruno also knew that leaving the flock unattended for any length of time could have spelled even bigger disaster if a pack of coyotes came along.

Bruno's solution? He'd stand on a small overlook for about five minutes, surveying the flock in the valley below and scanning the surrounding hillsides for any sign of movement by a coyote or another predator, and then head over to the mama in labor. He'd lie right beside her until the lamb was out and on the ground, at which point he'd lick the lamb clean and eat the afterbirth from the delivery so that the scent of blood wouldn't attract a passing predator. Once he saw that the new lamb was up on its feet, nursing, and that the new mom had accepted the baby and was bonding with the new arrival, Bruno would trot a little ways to a spot on the high ridge where he could see the rest of the flock in the valley. When he saw that the flock was safe, he'd trot back to mama and baby and hunker down beside them until it was time to check on the flock again.

He'd keep this up until my wife or I came out to gather the lamb and its mother and take them to our fenced-in nursery. Thanks to Bruno's diligent devotion to his job—his purpose—he figured out the perfect solution, down to the smallest detail.

And as for optimism, Bruno has enough to spare. No matter how rough a night he's endured out in the unpredictable and sometimes brutal weather conditions of Colorado, when he sees you, he always greets you with a wagging tail and that big happy smile of his. Any time of day or night, you can walk out to where the flock is grazing or resting and Bruno will stand up and smile that ear-to-ear smile and look at you as if to say, "I'm so happy to see you. And thank you for the opportunity to guard your sheep."

All of Bruno's strengths are impressive in themselves, but what pushes them over the top and makes Bruno greater than the sum of his parts—a positive beacon of light for those sheep—is his sense of purpose. He's as loyal a servant to our sheep as they come, and it's because he has absolute clarity about his role in life. If he didn't, what would he apply all those wonderful qualities to? He'd be a servant without a master, simply adrift. His purpose is what gives his life and his gifts and talents meaning.

In Chapter 1, I said my mother was the inspiration for the writing of this book, as she embodied the eight character traits I've been talking about. Her unwavering faith in God and her eternal positive outlook on life kept her smiling even in the face of seemingly insurmountable odds. The fact that she went back to school full time while working to support two young children was proof of her discipline, flexibility and tenacity. And imagine the resilience required to land on your feet after confronting the harsh reality that you've suddenly become a forty-six-year-old single mom with no job, no house, no car and no money.

I believe that what allowed my mom to rise up and prevail during the most difficult time of her life was purpose. She knew without question what her purpose in life was. She was put on this earth to raise her two children to be the best they could possibly be, to make sure my sister and I had the strength of character and intestinal fortitude to succeed in any situation. Mom had a calling that outweighed any hardship, and that calling was to empower her children.

I'm a little older than Mom was when she became a widow, and I find my thoughts turning more and more to the purpose of *my* life. Much of the past twenty-five years of my life has been spent seeking the next adrenaline rush or trying to figure out how to make another dollar. I've driven race cars on the fastest tracks in the world, piloted my own airplanes, dredged for gold in the hills of northern California, and started and grown multiple businesses. For many years, I'd assumed that my purpose in life was to make as much money as possible as quickly as possible and have some thrills along the way, and that's where I invested my efforts. But in that race to the next big thing or the next hundred dollars, I never *really* thought about my purpose. I never looked beneath the surface for my life's deeper meaning.

As I've gotten older, I've come to realize that my focus on money, fame and adrenaline wasn't in focus at all. The light in my young eyes was just a refracted vision seen through a prism of superficial aspirations. My out-of-focus purpose was working in direct conflict with God's plan for my life. I now realize that no matter how much money or power you have and no matter how much recognition you get, it's impossible to be happy in your professional or personal life until the direction you're headed in is in agreement with God's purpose for your life.

The word *purpose* can have different meanings to different people. For me, it means a calling that's bigger than one's own selfish desires. To live your purpose, you have to shift your focus from your personal desires for your life to the plans that God has for your life. And there has to be a significant shift in trust as well. Many successful people trust only themselves. They believe they've reached those pinnacles through their own strength, and they don't trust anyone else to help them move forward in life. But to find your true purpose, you have to shift your trust from yourself to God, and this is hard for successful, confident people to do.

For almost four years, this book has been a purpose for me and, I believe, a part of God's plan. At first I didn't have enough trust in myself to sit down and write it. Who would read a book that *I* wrote? But one day, the calling finally became too strong. I gave in to God's purpose, put my fingers on the keyboard and let Him take over. And here I am just a few paragraphs from the end of the book.

But what about my other purposes? I believe we can transition from one purpose to another as we move through our lives and as God's plans for us change. Life is a very fluid state of affairs. Human needs change and God's needs change, sometimes on a daily basis. I also believe that God can have more than one purpose for us simultaneously. We may have a purpose in our personal lives, such as raising children or taking care of elderly parents or teaching a Sunday-school class, at the same time as we are called for another purpose in our professional lives.

Unfortunately, despite the potential for multiple purposes, many people can't identify even one. They're like a ship without a sail, an airplane without a rudder or a GPS without an address to work with. They have no direction, no heading, no wind in their sails, and there's no land in sight.

No matter your position, you should know your purpose and come to work every day with that purpose firmly in hand like a compass to guide your day. Whether you're the farmer, the mule or the plow, there's no doubt that your life has a purpose.

Imagine if the CEO and all the vice presidents, directors, managers, department heads, customer-service reps and administrative assistants came to work every day with a common purpose. Imagine if they all realized their purposes and were all working toward a common goal for the good of the company. There would be nothing they couldn't accomplish.

Give *your* purpose some thought. Think about how your professional purpose might fit in with the goals and the purpose of the entire organization. CEOs and vice presidents, I want you to consider whether you've adequately conveyed the overall purpose of your organization to your employees. Directors, managers and departments heads, look deep into your departments and ask yourself, "Do the people I lead really know their purpose? Have I effectively conveyed that purpose so that we're all working toward a common goal?" And as for the rank-and-file employees who give their lives, one heartbeat at a time, to keep the company moving forward, ask yourselves, "Do I know my purpose?" We all have a purpose that we owe it to ourselves to discover.

Imagine if we all had the level of conviction about our purposes in life that Bruno does. Imagine how influential we could be with the flocks we guard in our own lives every day. Imagine how much more powerful our diligence, tenacity, optimism, flexibility, discipline, resilience, confidence and purpose would be if we greeted every morning—having survived the previous day's blizzard—with big Bruno smiles on our faces, eager for whatever the day holds because we know we have a purpose much greater than ourselves. Imagine how much more likely our flocks would be to follow us to the ends of the earth if they could see that purpose in us. That's powerful stuff!

We'd all do well to be more like Bruno. There's no question that if you go to work every day with a true purpose, with a direction, with the optimism to face a new day, your life will take on new meaning. You'll be more motivated and more productive, and your days will be more fulfilling than you've ever imagined. I guarantee it.

So look deep inside yourself and ask, "What's my purpose in life?" The answer is there—you just have to look for it. And it's worth looking for. You'll never make a more important discovery.

A CLOSING NOTE

SUCCESS IS ACHIEVABLE!

Whatever your personal definition of it is, success in life is right there for the taking. God wants you to be successful. He's given you opportunities in your life, some of which you've accepted and made the best of. Maybe you've intentionally ignored other opportunities or didn't see them for what they were, diamonds in the rough, opportunities hidden in an opaque shell.

I've always thought our opportunities for success are like a series of windows on a rotating carousel, windows that open and close as the carousel of life rotates past us. Some of these windows of opportunity are hung low, where they're easy for us to reach. We may be able to walk up and peek into them, testing the waters in a sense before we take the leap of faith inside. Other windows are hung higher, reachable with a little effort. Most of us believe we can reach them, but others don't take advantage of the opportunity. They don't make the effort required to reach that level of success.

Still other windows are hung *much* higher on the carousel, so high that they look almost impossible to reach. But even these can be reached. It just takes a better plan and a little grit in your craw.

As we stand and watch the carousel, our success is right there in front of us, waiting just behind those windows of opportunity. Though some of them are harder to reach than others, they're all right there, inviting us in before they close. And the choice is ours—a choice very similar to the choice we make when we walk into our offices every day. Will we take advantage of the window that's beckoning to us, regardless of how high it's hung, or will we watch it pass by, never to open to us again?

Sure, it will take a little effort on your part to climb up onto that carousel and seize that brief moment of opportunity, but like my mother said, when you turn the corner on any hardship, the blessings on the other side far outweigh the pain and suffering you endured to get there. And like Proverbs 13:4 says, "The soul of the sluggard craves and gets nothing, while the soul of the diligent is richly supplied."

If the window you aspire to reach is the one at the top of the carousel, the one that seems so far out of reach, all you have to do is embrace the eight qualities I've focused on in this book and make them a part of your daily routine. Success doesn't come easily—it comes

A Closing Note

through a calculated, deliberate, mode of operation in your daily life—and these eight qualities will act as a foundation for that success. If exercised diligently and with a tenacious spirit, they'll take you to the next level in your career and in your personal life. They'll take you to the top of the carousel, where you can jump through the window that's offering you the opportunity to achieve your greatest ambitions.

I wish you the very best in your pursuit of the success you desire in life. I hope the values and lessons I've shared with you will play a role in your daily life and help you to focus on your true purpose and live it. Success can be yours—God has given you the opportunity—so don't miss the window. Climb up there on that carousel and seize your success!

ACKNOWLEDGMENTS

Thank you to Dr. Grace T. Edwards and to Dr. John C. Nemeth for your support, guidance and advice during all phases of this project.

Thank you to my dear friends and colleagues within the Southern Farm Bureau Life Insurance Company. The positive influences you have had in my life are immeasurable and I am truly thankful for the relationships we have built over the years. A special thank you to David Hurt and E.J. "Bubby" Trosclair for the confidence you have placed in me and for the opportunities you have given me to grow as a professional. I am blessed to represent such a wonderful company. And thank you to my friends within the North Carolina Farm Bureau and South Carolina Farm Bureau Insurance Companies for the confidence in me that you showed by hiring me as an agent and for the training and support you gave me.

A special thanks to my editor, Doug Wagner of Windword Literary Services, who helped to bring clarity to my thoughts and structure to my sentences and to make this book flow so smoothly. You did an awesome job, my friend!

Most of all, I thank God for His countless blessings in my life. I am thankful for the leadership, guidance and direction He has given over the many courses of my life. Without His blessing and inspiration, the crafting of this book would not have been possible. To Him be all the glory for this work.

ABOUT THE AUTHOR

Robert Luckadoo has a knack for success. Whether it's in the world of NASCAR racing, collegiate fast-pitch softball or financial services, he's always found a way to win. It's no wonder that audiences find him to be such an inspiring speaker.

A geophysics major with a master's in business management, Robert started his first company—a geological consulting firm—in 1989, and since then he's become something of a startup expert, starting six more businesses and growing them to maturity before selling them for profit as going concerns. Currently, he's a financial professional with Southern Farm Bureau Life Insurance Company and has a reputation for commitment and integrity and a lengthy history of customer satisfaction within the financial-services industry. Because he considers helping clients with their financial needs to be a high calling, word of mouth has always been very much in his favor.

And Robert's track record literally extends to the track. He's a former team owner and driver in the NASCAR Goody's Dash and Winston Racing series, and in 1997 he finished in the top fifteen as a rookie in the Discount Auto Parts 250 at Daytona International Speedway and twelfth in the final NASCAR Goody's Dash Series points standings. His love of sports and his leadership skills have also led him to coaching positions in fast-pitch softball at the University of North Carolina at Chapel Hill and at Meredith College in Raleigh, N.C., where he transformed the Avenging Angels team from cellar dwellers to conference contenders.

In recent years, Robert has added "inspirational speaker" to his resume and written his first book, *Grit in Your Craw: The 8 Strengths You Need to Succeed in Business and in Life*. Both of these avenues have allowed him to share the lessons that success has taught him with thousands of people.

When he isn't working, Robert is likely to be outside. Whether it's on a golf course, a hiking trail, or in his boat on a well-stocked southern reservoir, he and his wife Paula enjoy spending time together in the great outdoors.

ROBERT WANTS TO HEAR FROM YOU!

I WOULD LOVE TO HEAR your personal stories of success! If you have a story you would like to share, please email me at:
Robert@robertluckadoo.com

If you need a little more "Grit in YOUR craw," check out my website:
www.robertluckadoo.com

While you're there, take a look at my Blog for additional motivational messages and inspirational stories.
And, don't forget to sign up for my email list!
You can also follow me on Twitter:
@robert_luckadoo